THE ROLLING STONES

Celebrating 50 Years of the
Greatest Rock and Roll Band in the World

10648004

THE
ROLLING
STONES

Celebrating 50 Years of the
Greatest Rock and Roll Band in the World

Photographs from the

Daily Mail

ATLANTIC WORLD

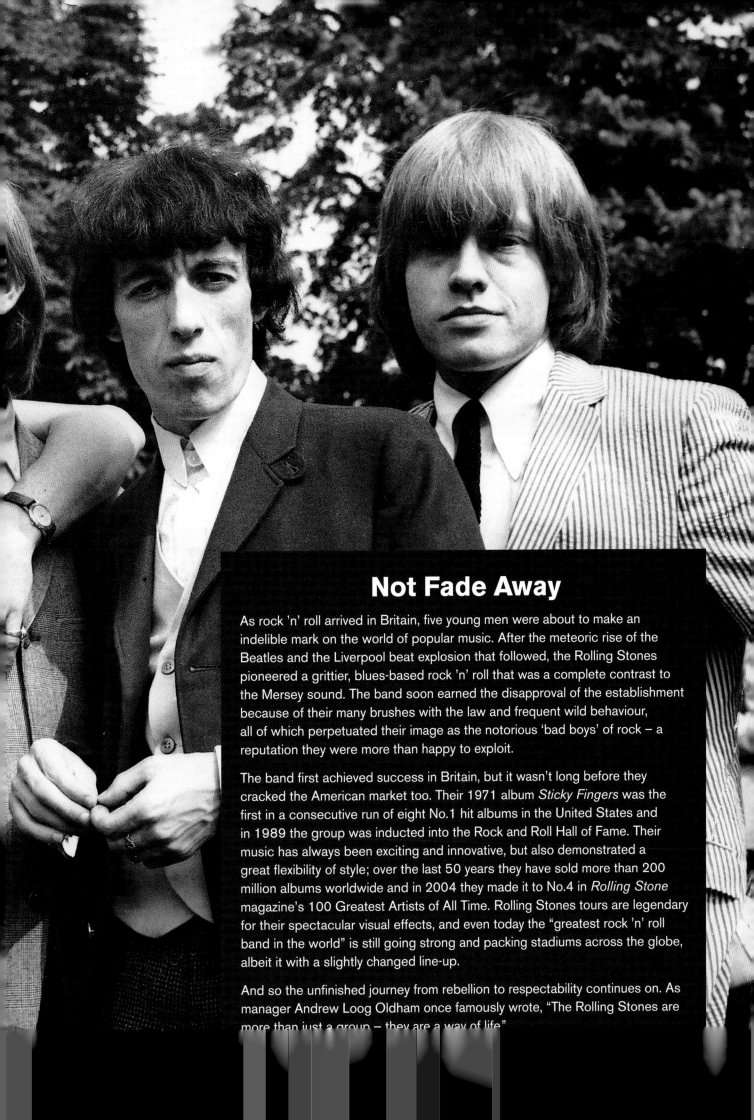

Not Fade Away

As rock 'n' roll arrived in Britain, five young men were about to make an indelible mark on the world of popular music. After the meteoric rise of the Beatles and the Liverpool beat explosion that followed, the Rolling Stones pioneered a grittier, blues-based rock 'n' roll that was a complete contrast to the Mersey sound. The band soon earned the disapproval of the establishment because of their many brushes with the law and frequent wild behaviour, all of which perpetuated their image as the notorious 'bad boys' of rock – a reputation they were more than happy to exploit.

The band first achieved success in Britain, but it wasn't long before they cracked the American market too. Their 1971 album *Sticky Fingers* was the first in a consecutive run of eight No.1 hit albums in the United States and in 1989 the group was inducted into the Rock and Roll Hall of Fame. Their music has always been exciting and innovative, but also demonstrated a great flexibility of style; over the last 50 years they have sold more than 200 million albums worldwide and in 2004 they made it to No.4 in *Rolling Stone* magazine's 100 Greatest Artists of All Time. Rolling Stones tours are legendary for their spectacular visual effects, and even today the "greatest rock 'n' roll band in the world" is still going strong and packing stadiums across the globe, albeit it with a slightly changed line-up.

And so the unfinished journey from rebellion to respectability continues on. As manager Andrew Loog Oldham once famously wrote, "The Rolling Stones are more than just a group – they are a way of life."

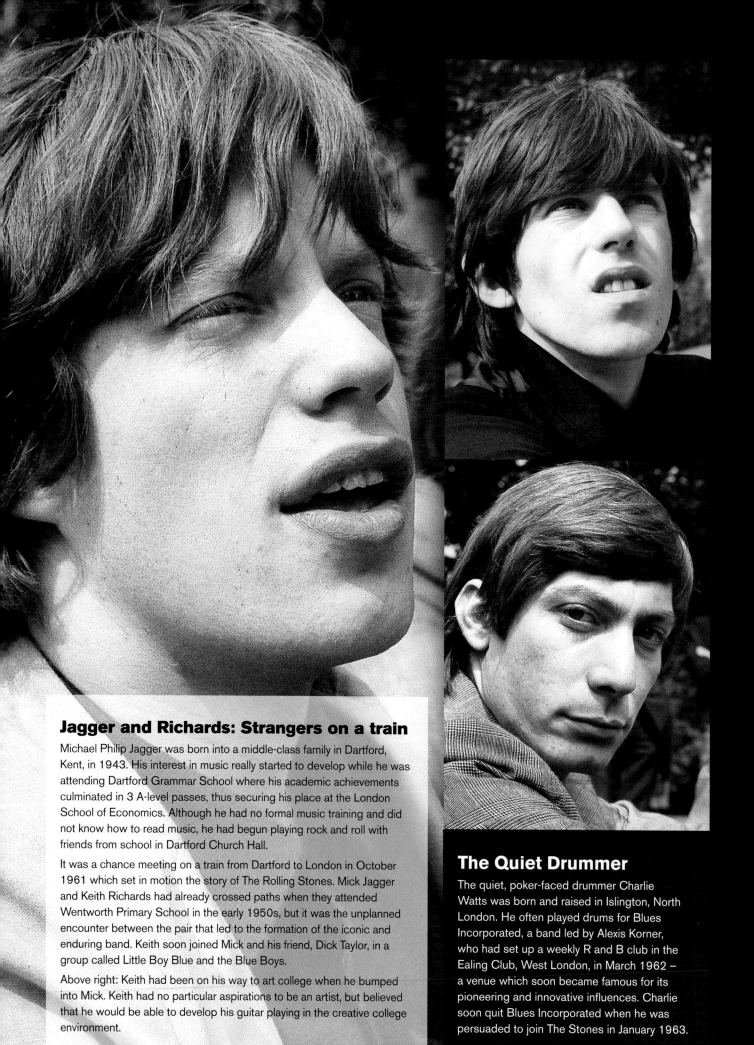

Jagger and Richards: Strangers on a train

Michael Philip Jagger was born into a middle-class family in Dartford, Kent, in 1943. His interest in music really started to develop while he was attending Dartford Grammar School where his academic achievements culminated in 3 A-level passes, thus securing his place at the London School of Economics. Although he had no formal music training and did not know how to read music, he had begun playing rock and roll with friends from school in Dartford Church Hall.

It was a chance meeting on a train from Dartford to London in October 1961 which set in motion the story of The Rolling Stones. Mick Jagger and Keith Richards had already crossed paths when they attended Wentworth Primary School in the early 1950s, but it was the unplanned encounter between the pair that led to the formation of the iconic and enduring band. Keith soon joined Mick and his friend, Dick Taylor, in a group called Little Boy Blue and the Blue Boys.

Above right: Keith had been on his way to art college when he bumped into Mick. Keith had no particular aspirations to be an artist, but believed that he would be able to develop his guitar playing in the creative college environment.

The Quiet Drummer

The quiet, poker-faced drummer Charlie Watts was born and raised in Islington, North London. He often played drums for Blues Incorporated, a band led by Alexis Korner, who had set up a weekly R and B club in the Ealing Club, West London, in March 1962 – a venue which soon became famous for its pioneering and innovative influences. Charlie soon quit Blues Incorporated when he was persuaded to join The Stones in January 1963.

Musical Wyman

Right: Bill Wyman, born William George Perks in Lewisham, London, in 1936, was the oldest member of the band. He attended Beckenham and Penge Grammar School for Boys, where he took piano lessons, joined the choir and played the clarinet. He learned to play the guitar during his National Service and this spell in the army also gave rise to his adopted surname, Wyman, the name of one of the friends who served with him at the time.

Rollin' Stones first gig

The original line-up of The Rolling Stones consisted of lead-vocalist Mick Jagger, guitarists Keith Richards, Brian Jones and Bill Wyman, drummer Charlie Watts and pianist Ian Stewart; the band's name was inspired by the 1950s Muddy Waters song, "Rollin' Stone".

The newly formed group played their inaugural gig using this name at London's Marquee Club on 12 July 1962. The Rollin' Stones soon morphed into The Rolling Stones. As the band became established they were signed up by the flamboyant impresario Andrew Loog Oldham after he saw them perform at The Crawdaddy Club in Richmond, Surrey, in April 1963. The 19-year-old manager soon dispensed with pianist Ian Stewart, informing the band that six members would be too many for a pop group. Stewart remained with the band as road manager and occasional keyboard player until his death in December 1985.

Brian Jones joined the band after he was spotted by legendary jazz musician Alexis Korner. Setting the pattern for his unconventional life, he had fathered two children with different women by the time he was 17. However, his love of music was evident at an early age – his mother taught him to play the piano when he was very young and he had the ability to pick up and play many instruments.

Above: This very early picture of the band belies the image they were soon to cultivate with such vigour. Their first appearance on ABC-TVs *Thank Your Lucky Stars* was the only time the group appeared wearing identical outfits. Soon they would be famous for their eclectic, rather bedraggled style, which they combined with wild and energetic stage performances – leading to manager Andrew Oldham's famous comment, "Would you let your daughter go out with one?"

Opposite right: Mick and Keith go shopping in Carnaby Street, London. Shortly after signing the group Andrew Oldham managed to negotiate a recording contract with Decca – the British record company which famously turned down the chance to sign The Beatles. In June 1963 The Stones' first single "Come On" was released. This Chuck Berry cover, backed with Muddy Waters' "I Want To Be Loved", made it into the UK charts at number 21.

Below: The band, seen here at the Montreux Television Festival in spring 1964, were now high-profile celebrities and as such were invited to many media events. They had embarked on their first UK concert tour in September 1963. Soon after this they released their second single, the Lennon-McCartney composition, "I Wanna Be Your Man". This gritty rendition reached number 12 in the UK charts and truly brought them to the attention of the record-buying public.

Keith uses the back stairs at London Airport to evade over-enthusiastic fans as The Stones set off for their first US tour in June 1964. After the success of the single "Not Fade Away" and the release of their debut album, *The Rolling Stones*, at the end of 1963 the band was riding high. Their two concerts at Carnegie Hall in New York were a huge hit and they were as well received in the States as they had been in Britain.

In June 1963 The Stones released their first single, a cover version of Chuck Berry's "Come On", which reached No. 21 in the UK charts.

Mick in court

Right: Mick Jagger leaves a Liverpool court with co-manager Eric Easton after pleading guilty to three motoring offences. His licence was endorsed and he was fined £32 but he escaped disqualification from driving. Easton came to work with Andrew Oldham after Beatles manager Brian Epstein had turned down Oldham's suggestion that they manage the group together. Mick was soon appearing in the gossip columns and dating Chrissie Shrimpton, sister of the model Jean Shrimpton. However, 1964 was also a productive year for the band as they had completed four UK and two US tours. They also celebrated their first UK number 1 single, "It's All Over Now", in July of that year.

The Jagger-Richards writing partnership was becoming more prolific, providing material for their own use and for other artists.

Above: The Stones were no strangers to controversy and had been dogged with a history of problems at live concerts. They had first experienced difficulties at Wembley Stadium in April 1964 when 30 fans were arrested for riotous behaviour and there were further issues in Scotland later in the year. This concert in Berlin in June 1965 was marred by rioting fans and 50 rows of seats were destroyed.

Song-writing partnership

Opposite: An early picture of the Stones performing. The band's first number 1 single was followed swiftly by an equally successful EP "Five by Five" released in August and another chart-topping blues song, "Little Red Rooster", in November 1964. By this time the Jagger-Richards writing partnership was becoming more prolific, providing material for their own use and for other artists. Gene Pitney's recording of "That Girl Belongs to Yesterday" was the first song composed by The Rolling Stones songwriting duo to become a top-10 hit in the UK.

1963 Timeline

Jan   Charlie Watts' recruitment persuades Bill Wyman to enlist with the group. First demo recordings are cut but no record label offers a contract.

Apr   The Beatles see the band in a Richmond, Surrey club and a friendship is forged while socialising in the Chelsea flat shared by Mick and Keith. Andrew Loog Oldham decides to manage the band.

10 May   Oldham produces the first cut of 'Come On' – destined to become the Stones' first single.

18 May   Journalist Norman Jopling files the first national rave review of the band.

7 Jun   'Come on/I Wanna Be Loved' is released on Decca, reaching No.21 in the British charts in August. For their first TV appearance the Rolling Stones all wear the same neat clothes. The band continues to perform at small clubs, private parties and halls. More TV appearances follow throughout the summer.

29 Sept   The Rolling Stones' first tour begins at the Victoria Theatre in London, the band supporting Bo Diddley and the Everly Brothers.

1 Nov   A second single, 'I Wanna Be Your Man', a Lennon/McCartney composition, is released. It enters the charts on 8 November and remains there for thirteen weeks, reaching No. 12.

28 Nov   The Stones meet American singer Gene Pitney. Three weeks later his record 'That Girl Belongs to Yesterday', written by Jagger and Richards and produced by Loog Oldham, begins its UK chart ascent.

20 Dec   The Rolling Stones are voted sixth best British small group in a *New Musical Express* poll.

The Stones received their award for Best British Band at a Variety Club of Great Britain luncheon at London's Savoy Hotel in September 1964.

5,000 fans storm the stage

Throughout 1964 the band toured triumphantly and another EP, "Five by Five", released in August kept fans happy. In September they were voted most popular group in a Melody Maker poll and 'Not Fade Away' was declared best single of the year. On 13 September in Liverpool, in an eerie preview of something that would take place in California many years later, the Stones had hired twenty-four rugby players to protect them at a concert. But some 5,000 fans still stormed towards the stage and overcame the guards. Four days later police dogs had to control 4,000 fans in Carlisle. On a sweeter note, Andrew Loog Oldham was married in Glasgow that month and Charlie wed Shirley Ann Shephard in Bradford a few weeks later.

The Stones were voted the best
British band in a *Melody Maker*
poll and "Not Fade Away" was also
named as best single of the year.

1964 Timeline

6 Jan The Rolling Stones' second British tour opens in Harrow, north-west London.

17 Jan An EP (extended play) is released, featuring five tracks. It spends eleven weeks in the singles charts, reaching No.15.

8 Feb Another UK tour begins, in London. It will close on March 7, just as the band's new single 'Not Fade Away', is released in the UK and the US.

16 Apr Decca release their first album, The Rolling Stones. On 24 April it reaches No.1 in the British album charts.

1 May A third UK tour begins, the day before 'Not Fade Away' enters the US charts. The single remains there for 13 weeks but does not achieve a high placing.

12 May The band are refused lunch in a Bristol hotel because they are not wearing ties.

19 May Riots in Hamilton, Scotland, as police attempt to calm 4,000 fans – some with forged tickets – who storm a gig at a local hotel.

27 May A Coventry headmaster suspends eleven boys who wear their hair like Jagger's.

1 Jun The band fly to New York for their first American tour. More than 5,000 fans greet them at Kennedy airport.

5 Jun First US concert in San Bernardino, California. A few days later they fail to fill a stadium in San Antonio, where locals profess to prefer their high school band. However, in other cities over the next few weeks the Stones are greeted rapturously.

23 Jun British fans riot at London airport as the band returns.

24 Jun Rolling Stones voted best British vocal band in a Record Mirror poll.

26 Jun 'It's All Over Now' is released and enters the British singles charts a week later at No. 7, making No. 1 soon afterwards.

8 Jul Mick, Keith and Bill attend a party at London's Dorchester Hotel following the premier of the Beatles' film A Hard Day's Night.

24 Jul A new British tour opens in Blackpool. Thirty of the 7,000 fans present, and two policemen, are injured in the crush.

31 Jul A concert in Belfast is abandoned after twelve minutes as hysterical girls are lifted away in straight-jackets.

6 Aug The Rolling Stones record an appearance for a networked American TV show. The next day they return to their roots and perform at the Richmond Jazz and Blues Festival, and then record for ITV's seminal Ready, Steady, Go television programme.

14 Aug The EP 'Five by Five' is released by Decca, recorded in Chicago in June. It is in Britain's singles' chart within days.

Marianne Faithfull's single 'As Tears Go By' is released.

5 Sept A new British tour begins at the Finsbury Park Astoria in London.

10 Sept The Rolling Stones are voted best British band in a Melody Maker poll. 'Not Fade Away' is voted best single.

13 Sept Thousands of fans are restrained by rugby players hired as a 'human shield' at a concert in Liverpool.

16 Sept Andrew Loog Oldham, 20, marries an eighteen year-old painter, Sheila Klein in Glasgow. The next day police dogs are required to control fans at a concert in Carlisle. In Edinburgh some days later, armoured cars are on standby to protect band members from excited fans.

9 Oct The album 12 x 5 is released in the USA, two days before the tour finishes in south London.

14 Oct Charlie Watts marries Shirley Ann Shephard in Bradford, Yorkshire.

17 Oct 'Time Is On My Side' enters the US charts at No. 80. It will remain there for thirteen weeks without becoming a major hit.

18 Oct The band is banned from appearing on Belgian TV after 5,000 fans greeted them at the airport in Brussels. Two days later, French fans riot in Paris.

23 Oct The Rolling Stones fly to New York for their second US tour.

24 Oct Ed Sullivan promises his massive TV show audience that the Stones will never appear again. He professes to be shocked by them.

31 Oct After a further series of triumphant and controversial US dates and filming of their slot for the classic film Gather No Moss, the Stones greet loyal fans in San Bernardino and go on to many other gigs before the tour ends in November.

20 Nov Back in Britain the new single 'Little Red Rooster' goes straight to the top spot in the British charts. The band is simultaneously banned from a BBC radio programme for failing to honour an earlier booking.

12 Dec Brian denies rumours that he is leaving the group. The Stones have just been voted best R&B group in a British poll.

21 Dec Charlie Watts' book about Charlie Parker, Ode to a High Flying Bird, is published.

Crowd Trouble

Mick celebrates his 21st birthday on 26 July 1964 at a hotel in Preston. As he toasted the occasion with a glass of orange juice, the Stones cover of American singer-songwriter Bobby Womack's "It's All Over Now" was climbing the UK charts. It soon reached the number 1 slot, where it remained for five weeks.

Opposite inset: Crowd control continued to be a problem for the band; a few days before Mick's birthday festivities the Stones appeared at the Tower Ballroom in Blackpool and had to be rescued after rioting broke out during the show. They had to leave the stage, and all their equipment was smashed. In an effort to pre-empt similar trouble in Liverpool later in the year, the band hired 24 rugby players to protect them at the concert. However, thousands of fans still managed to overcome the guards and storm the stage.

Charlie weds

Right: Charles Robert Watts married Shirley Ann Shepherd at a secret ceremony in Yorkshire on 14 October 1964. Soon after the wedding Charlie had to leave Shirley behind as he embarked on the second US tour of the year. The couple first met at an Alexis Korner gig, before Charlie became famous, and they remain together today. They have one daughter, Seraphina Watts, born on 18 March 1968.

Mounting tensions

Right: The band relax between gigs in Scotland in June 1965, but rumours about their differences were spreading. During their third North American tour in May 1965 they recorded one of the most famous Jagger-Richards songs, "(I Can't Get No) Satisfaction". It soon went to number 1 in the States, where it spent four weeks at the top of the charts and established The Stones as a worldwide premier act. However, the tour was beset with problems causing tensions between Brian and Mick to escalate.

Above: Brian and Keith depart for New York for their second American tour in October 1964. The tour coincided with the release of their second US album *12 x 5* on 17 October. While in the States the band made their first nationwide TV appearance on *The Ed Sullivan Show*, when an estimated 70 million viewers watched their performance. Their raunchy style did not go down well with the older generation, prompting Ed Sullivan to promise that they would never appear on his show again. However, they returned six months later!

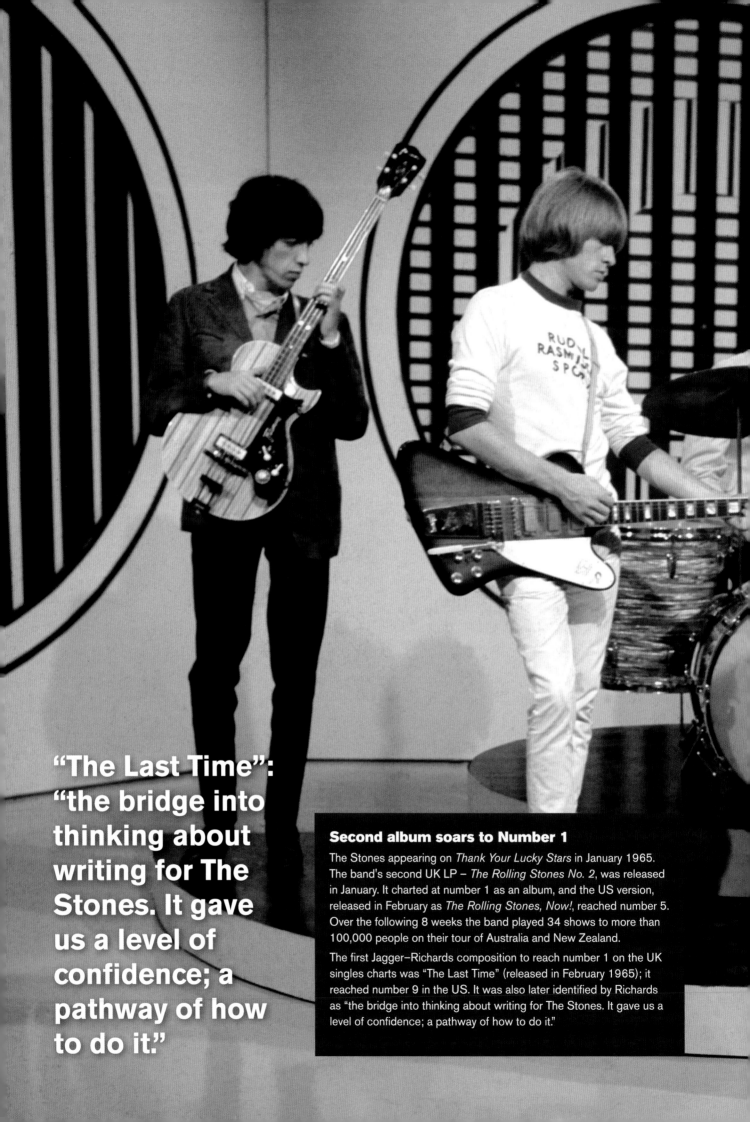

"**The Last Time**":
"**the bridge into thinking about writing for The Stones. It gave us a level of confidence; a pathway of how to do it.**"

Second album soars to Number 1

The Stones appearing on *Thank Your Lucky Stars* in January 1965. The band's second UK LP – *The Rolling Stones No. 2*, was released in January. It charted at number 1 as an album, and the US version, released in February as *The Rolling Stones, Now!*, reached number 5. Over the following 8 weeks the band played 34 shows to more than 100,000 people on their tour of Australia and New Zealand.

The first Jagger–Richards composition to reach number 1 on the UK singles charts was "The Last Time" (released in February 1965); it reached number 9 in the US. It was also later identified by Richards as "the bridge into thinking about writing for The Stones. It gave us a level of confidence; a pathway of how to do it."

1965 Timeline

15 Jan Rolling Stones No. 2, their second album, is released.

21 Jan The group arrive in Sydney, Australia. 3,000 fans welcome them.

22 Jan The new album enters British charts at No.1.

31 Jan The Rolling Stones fly to New Zealand after nine sell-out gigs in Melbourne.

15 Feb The group flies to Singapore.

17 Feb After the final tour date, in Hong Kong, the group flies to the USA.

26 Feb 'The Last Time' single is released. It will enter the charts at No. 8 and then hold the No. 1 position for four weeks.

5 Mar A two-week British tour begins.

18 Mar After the tour ends in Romford, Essex, there are complaints when Mick Jagger, Brian Jones and Bill Wyman urinate against a garage forecourt wall.

24 Mar The Rolling Stones begin a short Scandinavian tour in Denmark, and go on to West Germany and Paris.

22 Apr Start of the the Stones' third tour of North America.

26 Apr The group is forced to leave the stage in London, Ontario, after police turn off the power.

2 May The Rolling Stones appear again on the Ed Sullivan TV show in New York.

27 May 'Satisfaction' is released in the USA.

30 May Final date of the tour, in New York. Shortly afterwards, the Rolling Stones beat the Beatles into second place in an American pop poll.

11 Jun The EP (extended play) 'Got Live If You Want It' is released amidst rumours of Mick Jagger's plans to marry Chrissie Shrimpton.

15 Jun Beginning of a short tour of Scotland.

23 Jun Start of a Scandinavian tour, opening in Norway.

1 Jul It is reported that summonses have been issued against Wyman, Jones and Jagger for their alleged 'insulting behaviour' in Essex on the night of 18 March. On 22 July each would be fined £5.

10 Jul In a Radio Luxembourg poll the Stones are voted more popular than the Beatles. Their third album, Out Of Our Heads, is about to be released.

1 Aug Launch of Andrew Loog Oldham's Immediate record label.

20 Aug 'Satisfaction' is released in the UK, entering the charts at No.3 a week later. It will spend three weeks at No.1.

2 Sept Brian Jones, who has recently bought a house in Los Angeles, counters rumours that the group is planning to decamp to the USA, where they have been recording.

3 Sept The first of several shows in Dublin, Belfast and the Isle of Man, followed by a new tour of West Germany and Austria.

15 Sept Fans demolish fifty rows of seats at a hall in West Berlin and then vandalise a train. Four hundred riot police do battle with them. Thirty-two fans and six policemen need hospital treatment.

24 Sept Start of a 22-date British tour which coincides with the release of Out Of Our Heads.

1 Oct Bill Wyman denies rumours that he is quitting the group.

3 Oct Keith Richard and Mick Jagger are both injured by over-enthusiastic fans at a concert in Manchester.

22 Oct The single 'Get Off of My Cloud' is released.

29 Oct The Rolling Stones open their fourth North American tour in Montreal.

5 Nov 'Get Off Of My Cloud' is simultaneously No.1 in the UK and the USA.

14 Nov An American magazine, Blast, suggests that Mick Jagger is leaving the band, just as a new LP, December's Children, is released in the USA.

5 Dec The tour finishes in San Diego. Anita Pallenberg flies from London to join Brian who had denied their impending marriage the previous day.

10 Dec 'Satisfaction' is voted single of the year in a British music press poll and the band is named best R&B group and second best vocal group in the world.

After its release in May 1965 "Satisfaction" reached No.1 in the States, where it spent four weeks at the top of the charts and established The Stones as a worldwide premier act.

Mick and Keith's bad boy image

Below: Keith and Charlie enjoy a cup of tea outside a London magistrates' court in July 1965. The three other band members had been summonsed to face charges of insulting behaviour and using obscene language. Mick, Brian and Bill underlined their rebel credentials when they faced accusations of urinating against a wall in a petrol station after they had been refused permission to use the facilities.

Inset: Mick and Keith cheerfully leave the court after they had been fined £5. Despite their bad boy image 1965 was a very successful year for the band. Their chart-topping singles of the previous year were supplemented by three more number 1s in the UK – "The Last Time", "(I Can't Get No) Satisfaction" and "Get Off of My Cloud" were all huge hits. The year also saw their first number 1 album success in the US with *Out of Our Heads*.

Opposite: The Stones pictured at yet another airport. They had rolled from one tour to another with little respite in 1965. There were also major changes in the personal relationships of some members of the group. Brian became inseparable from model Anita Pallenberg after meeting her backstage at a gig in Munich in September. Meanwhile, Mick's two-year love affair with Chrissie Shrimpton was on the wane, despite rumours that the couple were considering marriage.

Aftermath rocketed to No.1 in the UK charts and "Paint it Black", released as a single in May 1965, became an instant No.1 on both sides of the Atlantic.

1966 Timeline

1 Jan   Ready, Steady, Go TV slot.

4 Feb   Release of single '19th Nervous Breakdown'.

12 Feb   The group flies to New York for TV appearances, going on to tour Australia and New Zealand.

1 Mar   Final tour date in Auckland. Later this month Cliff Richard will release the single 'Blue Turns to Grey', written by Jagger and Richard.

12 Mar   The last of 21 new tracks are recorded at the RCA Studios in Hollywood. Many will be included on the forthcoming album, Aftermath.

25 Mar   Beginning of a two-week European tour.

30 Mar   Fans in Marseilles take on the police as hysteria mounts during a concert. The group's first anthology album, Big Hits (High Tide and Green Grass) has been released.

15 Apr   Release of the classic album Aftermath. One track 'Goin' Home' runs for nearly twelve minutes – unprecedented in pop music. The album will spend seven weeks at No.1 in the British charts. The single 'Paint It Black' is released in the USA this month.

13 May   'Paint It Black' is released in the UK. It will chart for six weeks, reaching No.1. Keith Richard has bought Redlands, a moated house, in Sussex.

15 Jun   Despite a nervous collapse the previous day, Mick Jagger appears on a BBC chat show.

17 Jun   Chris Farlowe's single 'Out Of Time', written by Jagger and Richards, is released on Immediate Records.

23 Jun   The Stones arrive in New York for their sell-out fifth North American tour, staying on a chartered yacht in the harbour as so many hotels have declined to take their booking. A British newspaper had reported that the Stones would sue as these restrictions injure their reputations.

28 Jul   The tour closes in Hawaii, after which the band record in Hollywood and make TV appearances before taking holidays and returning to Britain.

25 Aug   Mick Jagger and Chrissie Shrimpton escape unhurt from a road accident near his Marylebone flat. His Aston Martin, however, received £700 worth of damage.

27 Aug   Having hurt his hand on holiday in north Africa, it is rumoured that Brian Jones will be unable to play for at least two months.

23 Sept   'Have You Seen Your Mother Baby, Standing In The Shadow' is released as the Rolling Stones' new single. Its picture sleeve (a novelty) depicts band members in drag and the record is banned by the BBC. Nonethless it enters the charts a week later, peaking at No.5.

24 Sept   Start of a new UK tour.

4 Nov   The album Got Live If You Want It is released in the USA, reaching No. 6 in a chart stay of 48 weeks. This month Brian Jones posed in Nazi regalia with Anita Pallenberg. Rumours of their forthcoming marriage persist as the band cuts material for a new album in a Paris studio.

10 Dec   The band are voted second-best in the world in two British polls. Later that month Mick Jagger and Chrissie Shrimpton part. He is involved with Marianne Faithfull by then. Shrimpton attempted suicide.

There were growing tensions within the group – particularly between Mick and Brian who appeared to be embroiled in a wrangle over leadership.

Aftermath

Below: Four of the Stones pictured in New York during their fifth American tour in July 1966. The tour was supported by their album, *Aftermath*. The acclaimed album was the first to feature only Jagger-Richards compositions as well as the first to be recorded entirely in the States. The album soon rocketed to number 1 in the UK charts; it included "Paint it Black", which was released as a single in May and became an instant number 1 on both sides of the Atlantic.

Mick and Marianne

Right: By the time his relationship with Chrissie Shrimpton ended in December 1966 Mick was involved with singer Marianne Faithfull, another of Andrew Oldham's protégés. Her career was launched with the Jagger-Richards composition, "As Tears Go By", in June 1964 which reached number 4 in the UK charts. Marianne had previously been married to artist John Dunbar, with whom she had a son, Nicholas, in 1965.

Let's Spend Some Time Together...

Opposite below: Mick photographed at the beginning of 1967 just after the release of controversial single "Let's Spend the Night Together" backed by the ballad "Ruby Tuesday". Although it created shockwaves in Britain, the song was not banned from the airwaves. However, the lyrics proved to be too much for the more conservative American public and when the band made their third appearance on *The Ed Sullivan Show*, they were instructed to change the words to "Let's Spend Some Time Together".

Leadership wrangle

Opposite top: Body language tells the story – 1967 could be perceived as the Stones "annus horribilis" as a series of drug-related charges dogged the band for much of the year. There were growing tensions within the group – particularly between Mick and Brian who appeared to be embroiled in a wrangle over leadership. Brian was also becoming increasingly debilitated after his split with Anita Pallenberg, who had immediately embarked on a relationship with Keith.

Below right: Mick Jagger is still smiling in May 1967. Despite their troubles the band continued with their heavy touring schedule. However, their reputation meant that they were closely scrutinised by customs officials wherever they travelled and the police abroad were less than sympathetic towards them.

Remanded on bail

Left and above left: Keith and Mick outside Chichester court on 10 May 1967, where they had been remanded on bail. Keith had been charged with allowing his premises to be used for the consumption of illegal substances in February 1967 whilst Mick, together with friend and art dealer Robert Fraser, faced the lesser charge of possession. Police had raided Redlands, Keith Richard's moated Sussex house, after the *News of the World* newspaper had erroneously reported that Mick Jagger had admitted taking LSD. In fact the reporter who penned the story had been talking to Brian Jones in a dimly lit night club and mistaken him for the lead singer of the band! The amphetamines that police found in the jacket said to belong to Mick were actually Marianne's but Mick insisted that he should take responsibility.

Above: Mick and Keith put a brave face on it as they leave Redlands for their court appearance. Brian Jones had also been due to visit Keith's home on the day of the arrest but was quickly telephoned and warned to stay away after the police arrived. However, his own London flat on Courtfield Road was raided on the same day as Jagger, Richards and Fraser appeared in court. Jones was also charged with possession of a number of illegal substances and allowing his home to be used for the consumption of drugs.

A quick break for the infamous pair as the court adjourned for lunch. Police had to clear a crowd of screaming fans out of the way before they could venture outside. Bill and Charlie were not involved in any of the court cases and were therefore able to spend some time working on their next album – eventually to be released at the end of 1967 as *Their Satanic Majesties Request*.

1967 Timeline

13 Jan 'Let's Spend The Night Together' is released. The single's B-side is the elegiac 'Ruby Tuesday'. Several US radio stations ban the record and Jagger has to sing 'Let's Spend Some Time Together' on an American TV show.

20 Jan Release of a new album, Between The Buttons – all tracks written by Jagger and Richard.

22 Jan The group appear on the family-orientated British TV variety show, Sunday Night At The London Palladium, but refuse to join other stars waving on the stage roundabout which traditionally closes the show.

4 Feb In Cannes, where Jagger attends the annual music business award ceremonies with Marianne Faithfull, the Rolling Stones are nominated best British act.

15 Feb Fifteen police officers raid Keith Richard's Sussex home armed with a warrant issued under the Dangerous Drugs Act.

Soon Jagger, Jones, Richard and various women friends head for Morocco, hoping to relax after the Sussex 'bust'. On the way, asthmatic Brian Jones is admitted to a French hospital with respiratory problems.

10 Mar Brian flies from Nice to hospital in London. By the time he is well enough to join the party in Marrakesh, Anita Pallenberg and Keith Richard have become lovers. Whilst Brian was out recording ethnic music the others flew home from Tangier via Madrid. They left no note.

18 Mar Brian returns to London. Jagger and Richard are issued with court summonses.

25 Mar A three-week European tour opens in Sweden and will include concerts in West Germany, Austria, Italy, France, Switzerland, Holland and Poland. There are tensions between the band and police and customs officials throughout as the Stones have increasingly become associated with crowd violence and alleged drug-related offences.

10 May After the first of a series of court appearances relating to the raid at his Sussex home, Keith Richard, and Mick Jagger, are remanded on bail. On the same day Brian Jones is arrested at home in Kensington for separate drug-related offences. He too is given bail.

15 Jun Jagger and Richard supply backing vocals for the Beatles' single 'All You Need Is Love'. A new compilation album, Flowers, is released this month.

27/28 Jagger and Richards' cases are heard at a court in Chichester, West Sussex. They are both given prison sentences and told to pay costs.

30 Jun Jagger and Richard are awarded bail and the right of appeal.

1 Jul A leader in The Times reflects surprising public outrage at the severity of their sentences.

7 Jul Without Brian, who is in the hospital with nervous strain, the other Rolling Stones record. Jones is well enough to join them on 12 July.

31 Jul In the Court of Appeal Mick Jagger is given a conditional discharge and Keith Richards' sentence is quashed.

18 Aug The single 'We Love You' is released.

26 Aug Mick and Marianne Faithfull join the Beatles at the Maharishi Marhesh Yogi's seminar in Wales.

14 Sept When the band members arrive in New York from London and Paris they are questioned by immigration officials about their drugs trials in England.

29 Sept The Rolling Stones part company with Andrew Loog Oldham.

15 Oct Bill Wyman applies for membership of the Royal Horticultural Society.

30 Oct Brian is sentenced to nine months' imprisonment for drug offences. He is released on bail from Wormwood Scrubs the next day and on 12 December his sentence is commuted to three years' probation.

27 Nov The album Their Satanic Majesties Request is released in the USA. It will be weeks before it is available in Britain.

12 Dec On the day of Brian Jones' reprieve the Rolling Stones are voted best British R&B group and second best vocal group in an NME poll.

14 Dec Their Satanic Majesties Request enters the UK album charts and remains there for nine weeks, reaching No.3. Brian Jones collapses and is rushed to a London hospital suffering from strain and exhaustion.

Free men

Above: On 29 June Keith Richards was given a one-year jail sentence and sent to Wormwood Scrubs prison together with Robert Fraser who received six months. Jagger was sentenced to three months imprisonment and dispatched to Brixton Prison. The next day the strain clearly shows when the pair were both bailed at £5,000 pending appeals against their convictions. Fraser spent four months in jail after his appeal was denied.

Support from the Establishment

Opposite right: Although many of the public felt that the men had "got what they deserved", there was a great deal of criticism in the press about the severity of the sentences imposed. *The Times* published a supportive editorial written by William Rees-Mogg entitled "Who Breaks a Butterfly on a Wheel". Most of the other newspapers followed suit and condemned the sentences – with the notable exception of the *News of the World*.

Right: Following the press attention the appeal was brought forward to 31 July. Keith was unable to attend as he was suffering from chickenpox and did not therefore hear the good news that his conviction had been quashed. Mick's relief is evident as his sentence was altered to a one-year conditional discharge.

Back in action

Opposite left: The Jagger-Richards partnership was back in action but the pair had much to think about on their release. Immediately after his discharge Mick took part in a televised debate on the programme *World in Action*. The Bishop of Woolwich, politician Lord Stow-Hill and William Rees-Mogg were among the guests. Many people were surprised by Jagger's ability to articulate his argument

Brian heads off to New York with Anita Pallenberg in September 1967. His drug trial took place a few months later in London. He was found not guilty of possessing cocaine and methedrine, but was convicted of cannabis possession and allowing his premises to be used for the consumption of illegal substances. He was initially given a nine-month prison sentence which was commuted to three years' probation on appeal and ordered to seek professional help.

Right: Mick and Marianne. Andrew Oldham had noticed Marianne at a party when she was just 17 years old and asked the Jagger–Richards pair to write a song for her, which resulted in the soulful ballad, "As Tears Go By".

Brian Jones played in his last live show with the band at Wembley Arena on 12 May 1968.

Brian's last show

On 12 May 1968 the group made a surprise appearance at the *NME* Poll Winners' Show at Wembley Arena and performed "Jumpin' Jack Flash" for the first time. The song was released two weeks later and flew straight to the top of the charts in the UK – the first number 1 single for The Stones for two years. This concert also marked Brian's last live show with the band as he continued to battle his demons.

"Jumpin' Jack Flash" has since reached iconic status; the band has played it during every tour since its release and it is the song most often played in concert. It has also been used in many films and television shows, including the 1986 Whoopi Goldberg comedy film of the same name. In fact the soundtrack includes two versions of the song; one by The Rolling Stones and a cover version by "Queen of Soul", Aretha Franklin.

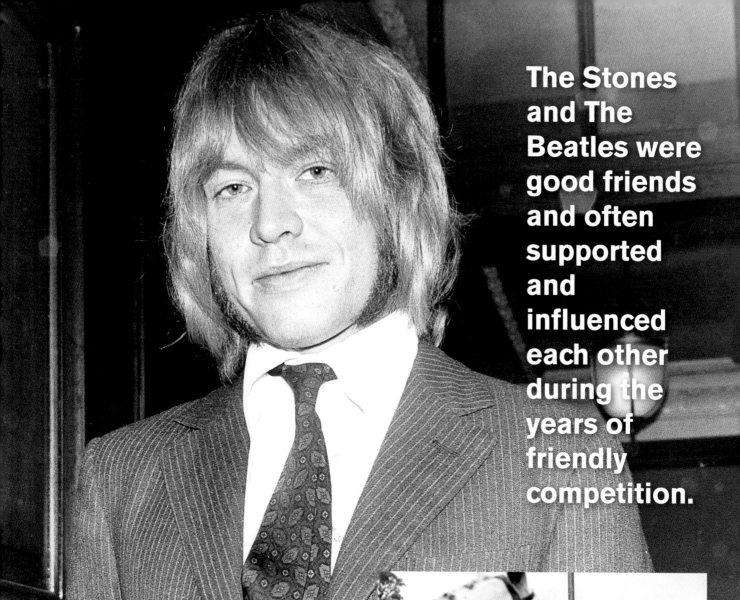

The Stones and The Beatles were good friends and often supported and influenced each other during the years of friendly competition.

Jones found guilty

Above: Brian had further run-ins with the law in May 1968 as he was again arrested on suspicion of possessing cannabis. He appeared in court on 26 September where he was found guilty of the charges and fined £50 plus costs. Although the sentence was surprisingly lenient for this second drug offence, it added to Brian's feelings of despair and depression.

Below: Brian with tour manager Tom Keylock and girlfriend Suki Poitier.

A different life for Charlie

Above: A pensive Charlie enjoys spending time on country pursuits with wife Shirley as the couple share a passion for horses. Shirley had studied sculpture at art college and still continues to pursue her interest as an amateur sculptor. She had once famously said of her introspective husband, "Charlie's not really a Stone, is he? Mick, Keith, Brian, they're the big bad Rolling Stones".

Friendly rivals

Left: Brian is pictured with John Lennon, Yoko Ono and John's son Julian in December 1968. Despite speculation about the rivalry between the two bands, they were in reality good friends and often supported and influenced each other during the years of friendly competition. Brian had played alto saxophone on the Beatles song "You Know My Name (Look Up the Number)", and Mick and Keith contributed to the backing vocals on the famous anthem "All You Need is Love". Lennon and McCartney had of course provided The Stones with their first top twenty hit, "I Wanna Be Your Man".

1968 Timeline

13 Mar The band are in the Olympic Studios in London, cutting a new album, work which will continue until 18 April.

18 Mar Shirley Watts gives birth to daughter Serafina.

11 May It is announced that Mick Jagger is to star in a film called The Performance.

21 May Brian Jones is arrested for possession of cannabis at home in Chelsea. He denies the charge.

25 May The classic single 'Jumpin' Jack Flash' is released. It will reach No. 1 in both the UK and the USA.

26 Jul The single 'Street Fighting Man', taken from the Stones' forthcoming album, is released in the USA.

17 Aug There is speculation that Eric Clapton will join the Rolling Stones now that the 'supergroup' Cream have disbanded.

24 Aug Disputes about the 'lavatorial' sleeve of the new album delay Beggars' Banquet's release.

3 Sept 'Street Fighting Man' is banned in Chicago after political demonstrations.

12 Sept As Mick Jagger begins work on his film, now called Performance, Marianne Faithfull's film Girl on a Motorcycle, co-starring Alain Delon, is premiered in London.

26 Sept In a London court Brian Jones is fined for possession of cannabis.

4 Oct Marianne Faithful happily announces her pregnancy. Six weeks later and nearly six months pregnant she is taken to a maternity home and loses her baby the next day. Mick Jagger reports that they are both very upset.

21 Nov Brian Jones buys Cotchford Farm in Sussex, formerly the home of A.A. Milne, creator of Winnie the Pooh.

27 Nov Fears that the Rolling Stones are to split gather even as the new album is released in North America.

5 Dec Beggars' Banquet is at last released in Britain, with an ironic sleeve spoofing an invitation to a formal party. It enters the charts days later, at No. 3 and remains there for twelve weeks without going higher.

7 Dec The Rolling Stones are voted best British R&B band in the NME's annual poll.

18 Dec On Keith Richard's twenty-fifth birthday he and Anita, Mick Jagger and Marianne fly to Brazil to discuss black and white magic with a mystic.

In court again

Above: Mick Jagger and Marianne Faithfull had hoped for a more peaceful year following the turbulent events of 1968 and Marianne's miscarriage in November. However, there were further troubles ahead for the glamourous couple as drug charges were brought against them after a police raid on their home in Cheyne Walk, Chelsea, on 28 May 1969. They appeared at Marlborough Street Magistrates' Court the next day to face charges of possession of illegal substances and they were released on bail until 23 June. The police had claimed that they had found heroin, LSD and marijuana on the premises though Jagger maintained that any drugs found had been planted. When the case finally came to court he was fined £200 for possession of cannabis.

On 8 June 1969 Mick, Keith and Charlie visited Brian at his home in Sussex – the band agreed to part company citing "musical differences".

On 8 June 1969 Mick, Keith and Charlie set off to visit Brian at his Cotchford Farm home in Sussex. Ostensibly the visit was to discuss the future of the band, but there was no surprise at the outcome of the visit as Brian and the band agreed to part company citing "musical differences". Two days later a 22-year-old veteran of John Mayall's Bluesbreakers, guitarist Mick Taylor, was recruited to replace Brian.

Right: Keith with girlfriend Anita Pallenberg. Keith and Anita had been together since March 1967 when some of the band travelled to Morocco on holiday in order to escape the furore over their drugs trial. During this trip the stormy relationship between Jones and Pallenberg escalated until Anita had had enough and embarked on an affair with Keith as Brian fell ill and was hospitalised.

Brian found dead

Below: A recently-divorced Bill with a friend at Brian's funeral. Within a month of Mick Taylor joining the band Brian Jones was dead. He had been found at the bottom of the swimming pool at his Cotchford Farm on the night of 2 July 1969. The official coroner's verdict on the incident was death by accidental drowning under the influence of drugs and alcohol, but there is still much debate and controversy surrounding his untimely death.The funeral took place in Brian's home town of Cheltenham on 10 July and all the Stones attended, except Mick who was filming in Australia.

Bottom: Shirley and Charlie Watts, she in the white mourning of eastern cultures, he in traditional black.

Brian Jones drowned in his Sussex swimming pool on the night of 2 July 1969.

The band had already planned a free concert to celebrate their re-formation for 5 July and decided to proceed with it. Inevitably it became an emotional memorial to Brian and remains one of rock 'n' roll's seminal occasions.

Introducing Mick Taylor

The new line up of The Rolling Stones featured the handsome, rather self-effacing Mick Taylor. Mick was born in Hatfield, Hertfordshire, on 17 January 1947 and had been inspired to play the guitar by one of his uncles. His presence in the band was a significant factor in the riff-driven sound that is now so indelibly linked with the Stones

1969 Timeline

4 Jan Brian Jones is reported to be 'furious' when hotels in Sri Lanka bar him in the mistaken belief that he is a drifter.

March The band return to Olympic Studios in London to cut a new album. Jagger and Richard work together on new songs, spending time writing in Italy in April.

24 May It is announced that Mick Jagger and Marianne Faithfull will star in an Australian film, Ned Kelly.

28 May After a police raid at Jagger's Chelsea home, he and Marianne are arrested for possession of cannabis. They are remanded and released on bail.

7 Jun Keith Richard's car is written-off after a crash near his home in Sussex. A heavily pregnant Anita Pallenberg sustains a broken collar bone but the baby is safe.

8 Jun Band members collect at Cotchford Farm and an amicable split is agreed with Brian Jones. Musical differences are cited.

10 Jun Mick Taylor is appointed as Jones' replacement.

1 Jul Drug charges against Mick Jagger and Marianne Faithful are adjourned until 29 September.

2/3 Jul The body of Brian Jones is lifted from the bottom of his swimming pool at Cotchford Farm. A coroner later reports that he had drowned under the influence of alcohol and drugs.

5 Jul A free Rolling Stones concert in London's Hyde Park goes ahead as planned. Thousands of white butterflies are released as Mick Jagger reads from Shelley in Brian's honour.

8 Jul Marianne Faithfull overdoses and falls into a long coma in Australia. Another actor takes over her part in Ned Kelly. 'Honky Tonk Women' enters the US and UK charts. Two weeks later it will be No.1 in Britain.

9 Jul The divorce of Bill and Diane Wyman is announced.

10 Jul Brian Jones is buried in Cheltenham.

13 Jul Mick Jagger starts work on Ned Kelly. Filming ends in September.

10 Aug Anita Pallenberg gives birth to a son, Marlon.

12 Sept Another compilation album, Through The Past Darkly (Big Hits Volume 2) is released. It reaches No.1 and will stay in the British charts for sixteen weeks.

17 Oct The Rolling Stones fly to Los Angeles to prepare for their first American tour in three years and to mix the next album, Let It Bleed. It will be released in Britain in December.

7 Nov This sixth American tour is a sell-out and opens in Colorado.

13 Nov Warner Bros waver about the US release of Performance because they find the English actors' accents 'unintelligible'.

28 Nov Let It Bleed goes on sale in the USA and the Rolling Stones are triumphant at a filmed Madison Square Gardens concert. Jimi Hendrix is backstage.

6 Dec At Altamont, California, the final concert of the tour descends into tragedy. Three fans die and many more are seriously injured.

8 Dec Back home Anita Pallenberg is informed that she must marry or leave England.

11 Dec Marianne Faithfull, who was in Italy with her son and a new friend during the recent tour, reunites with Mick Jagger.

19 Dec At a London court Mick Jagger is fined for possession of cannabis. Marianne Faithfull is acquitted.

21 Dec The band give two Christmas shows at a ballroom off the Strand, London.

Disaster at Altamont

Keith and Charlie return from the American tour of 1969, which was to end in tragedy. The Stones' final concert at Altamont in California on 6 December 1969 was intended to be the US equivalent of the band's free Hyde Park concert in England earlier in the year when the Hell's Angels had provided the security. Unfortunately at Altamont a young man named Meredith Hunter became involved in an altercation with some members of the gang and was stabbed to death. By the end of the concert three more people were dead and hundreds injured.

Ups and downs

Above: Jagger's introduction to acting in Nicholas Roeg's film *Performance* in 1968 had sparked his interest in films and in the summer of 1969 he and Marianne Faithfull travelled to Australia to film the movie *Ned Kelly*. Unfortunately the catalogue of troubles in his personal life continued when Marianne Faithfull took a massive overdose of sleeping pills and fell into in a coma for several days.

Below: Keith and Anita relax at their Chelsea home in December 1969, a few months after the birth of their son Marlon. The couple lived at 3 Cheyne Walk – a few doors down from Mick who lived at number 48. Despite constant enquiries about their plans, the couple never married although they remained together for many years.

Let It Bleed

Opposite and this page: The band, with new guitarist Mick Taylor, pose before their concert at the Saville Theatre in December 1969.The Stones had just released their new album *Let It Bleed*, a follow up to the 1968 album *Beggar's Banquet*. The new album was acclaimed by the critics and reached number 1 in the UK album charts, knocking the Beatles' *Abbey Road* off the top slot. Two of the tracks featured Brian Jones on autoharp. The surreal cover of the LP featured a grotesque cake designed by Robert Brownjohn, a graphic designer known for his work with sixties pop culture. This was the last album the Stones released on the Decca label.

In December 1969 *Let It Bleed* reached No.1 in the UK album charts, knocking the Beatles' Abbey Road off the top slot.

Jagger fined for possession

Mick tries to shield Marianne Faithfull from the huge crowd of photographers outside the London court where they had been summoned to appear on 19 December 1969. The couple pleaded not guilty to a charge of possessing cannabis but the case had been delayed several times while Jagger and Faithfull were in Australia filming *Ned Kelly*. Jagger was fined £200 for possessing cannabis and made to pay 50 guineas costs. The charges against Faithfull were dismissed.

Gimme the honky tonk girl

The band performs on stage at the Lyceum Ballroom in London on 21 December 1969. This was part of a mini-tour of the UK to round off the year before Mick travelled to Rome to try to rekindle his relationship with girlfriend Marianne Faithfull. 1969 had been a difficult and challenging year for The Stones, both personally and professionally. The group had undergone a change in line-up and they had cut back on touring to spend more time in the studio. It was some consolation that their sole single of the year, "Honky Tonk Women", and only album released, *Let It Bleed*, both reached number 1 in their respective UK charts.

Starring in Ned Kelly

Jagger and two other actors pose in Australian policemen's uniforms in a publicity shot for the movie *Ned Kelly* which starred Jagger in the title role. The film was directed by Tony Richardson and told the story of an Australian bushranger and folk-hero. There were many protests about the casting of Jagger as the legendary figure, both from Ned Kelly's descendants and from the actors' union Equity.

Farewell Marianne

Below left: Marianne was increasingly dependent on drugs by the end of 1969 and her relationship with Mick was soon to come to an end. Her personal life quickly went into decline and her career went into a tailspin. She resorted to living on the street and soon lost custody of her son as a consequence. She eventually made a successful comeback in the late 1970s when she re-invented herself as a smokey-voiced survivor.

Bianca Perez Morena

Left: Mick Jagger en route to Sweden during the band's 1970 European Tour. The series of concerts which started in Scandinavia on 30 August and finished in Amsterdam on 9 October, was the first in Europe since 1967.

Below: It was on this tour of Europe that Mick first met Bianca Perez Morena de Macia at a party after a concert. Bianca, who was born in Managua, Nicaragua, in 1945, was studying political science in the city after winning a university scholarship.

Farewell to Britain

Below: Mick Jagger in familiar pose on stage in the band's Farewell to Britain Tour in March 1971. Following this first tour in their homeland since 1966, the group announced that they were moving to the South of France. Although many theories were expressed about this defection, the band always denied that their decision had anything to do with tax avoidance. After endless discussions and clashes, The Stones' contract with Decca had finally expired in July 1970; they signed a deal with Atlantic Records which allowed them to release songs on their own Rolling Stones label. *Sticky Fingers*, issued in April, was their first release on the new label.

Right: Mick indulges his passion for cricket at a match in August 1972. The previous month, Mick had celebrated his 29th birthday at a party with celebrity guests including Truman Capote, Bob Dylan, Andy Warhol and Carly Simon. A few days later he announced that he would retire from rock 'n' roll at the age of 33.

In June 1971 the Stones topped the UK chart with the album Sticky Fingers and the single "Brown Sugar".

Left: Bill Wyman was far more circumspect than some other band members when it came to the use of alcohol and drugs, but was, by his own admission, "girl mad".

Above: Mick, Mick and Charlie in Paris. Rolling Stones fans had running fights with French police. Some fans had tried to crash the first of three Paris concerts without tickets.

1970 Timeline

14 Mar It is announced that the band's first European tour for three years will open in Holland in May and finish in Helsinki in early June. In fact, the tour is postponed for four months.

May Reports in the British press suggest that Brian Jones' debts were over five times greater than his assets. His estate may be due royalties from songwriting earnings.

24 Jun Ned Kelly is premiered in London.

28 Jun Mick Jagger is said to be dating American actress Patti D'Arbanville.

11 Jul Warner Brothers may shelve Performance.

31 Jul The Rolling Stones' contract with Decca expires. The band are set to launch their own record label.

6 Sept Release of the Get Yer Ya Ya's Out! album which reaches No.1 and remains in the charts for thirteen weeks.

10 Oct The day before the European tour ends in Munich, Mick Jagger visits London with a new girlfriend, the Nicaraguan Bianca Perez Morena de Macia.

20 Oct Mick Jagger, cited as co-respondent, is ordered to pay costs in John Dunbar's divorce from Marianne Faithfull.

6 Dec A documentary film, Gimme Shelter, covering the Stones' last American tour and featuring scenes from Altamont, is premiered in New York.

1971 Timeline

4 Jan British Premier of Performance.

6 Feb A farewell tour is announced amidst expectations that the band will become tax exiles in France. It opens in Newcastle and ends at the Roundhouse in north London.

26 Mar The Rolling Stones are filmed in performance for TV at the Marquee Club.

1 Apr The band gives a farewell party in Maidenhead before leaving for France. Band members take up residence in different but neighbouring houses.

15 Apr 'Brown Sugar' the Stones' next single, is featured on the BBC's Top of the Pops. It enters the charts a week later and will reach No.1.

23 Apr Release of the Sticky Fingers LP.

12 May Mick Jagger marries Bianca in a civil ceremony in St Tropez. Both wear white suits. The bride is several months pregnant.

28 May Keith has a road accident and will appear in court on subsequent assault charges. Gimme Shelter is screened in Cannes.

1 Jun The Rolling Stones top the British singles and album charts with 'Brown Sugar' and Sticky Fingers.

31 Jul British Premier of Gimme Shelter.

31 Aug The four surviving original Stones and Brian Jones' father launch a law suit against Andrew Loog Oldham about alleged irregularities relating to earnings derived through their original recording contract with Decca and other rights.

Oct The mixing of twenty new songs continues and the band plans a new album to coincide with next spring's American tour.

21 Oct Bianca Jagger gives birth to a daughter, Jade, in Paris.

Dec The band work on the new album at the Sunset Sound studios in Los Angeles.

3 Dec French magistrates accept Keith Richards' defence of self defence after the 'assault' that followed his road accident in May. Charges are dismissed.

15 Dec Decca release a double compilation album, Hot Rocks 1964–71.

Brown sugar 1970-71

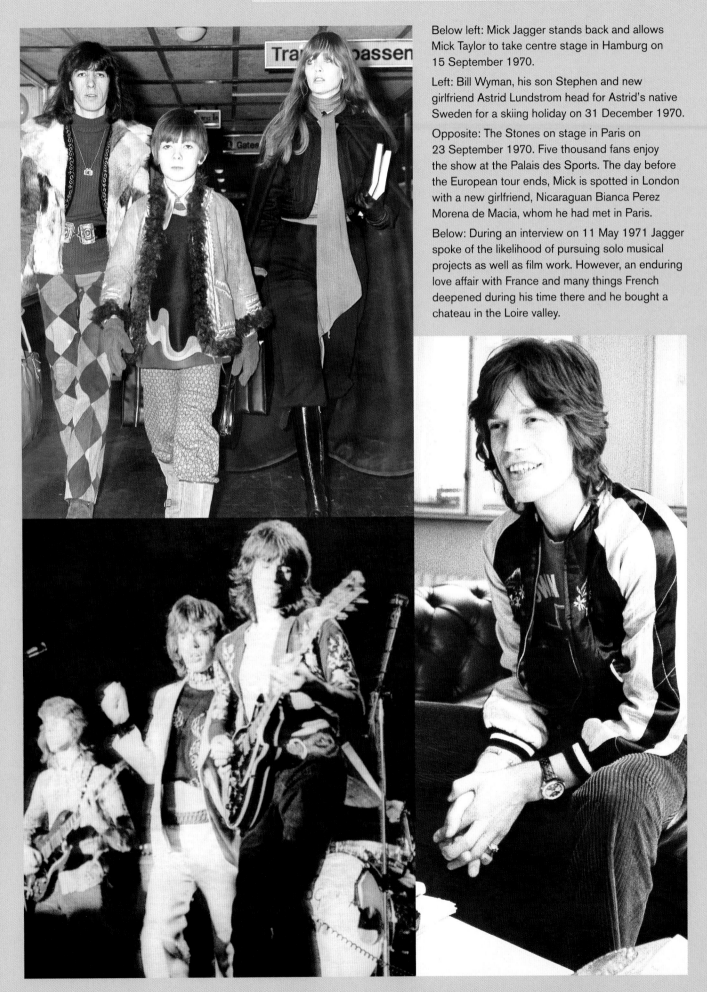

Below left: Mick Jagger stands back and allows Mick Taylor to take centre stage in Hamburg on 15 September 1970.

Left: Bill Wyman, his son Stephen and new girlfriend Astrid Lundstrom head for Astrid's native Sweden for a skiing holiday on 31 December 1970.

Opposite: The Stones on stage in Paris on 23 September 1970. Five thousand fans enjoy the show at the Palais des Sports. The day before the European tour ends, Mick is spotted in London with a new girlfriend, Nicaraguan Bianca Perez Morena de Macia, whom he had met in Paris.

Below: During an interview on 11 May 1971 Jagger spoke of the likelihood of pursuing solo musical projects as well as film work. However, an enduring love affair with France and many things French deepened during his time there and he bought a chateau in the Loire valley.

Goats Head Soup

Left: Mick strums an accoustic guitar in his Vienna hotel room as the group embark on their two-month European tour in September 1973. The tour followed the release of their latest album *Goats Head Soup* on 31 August. This was a follow-up to their *Exile on Main Street* LP, released in May 1972 and now hailed as a masterpiece. Both these albums topped both the UK and US album charts.

Probably the best known track on *Goats Head Soup* was the guitar-driven ballad "Angie", written mainly by Keith Richard. The single, released in August 1973, became a phenomenal success and was the band's first number 1 single in the US since "Honky Tonk Women" five years previously.

Above: Mick and Bianca photographed in London. The couple had married in St Tropez on 13 May 1971 when Bianca was four months pregnant. The ceremony was attended by celebrities including Paul and Linda McCartney, Ringo Starr and Eric Clapton and numerous photographers. The Queen's cousin, photographer Lord Lichfield, gave away the bride. The public were somewhat hostile towards Bianca and did not warm to her lofty detachment.

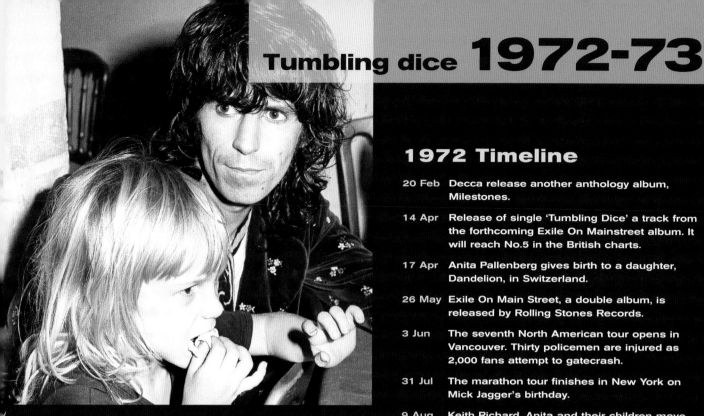

1972 Timeline

20 Feb Decca release another anthology album, Milestones.

14 Apr Release of single 'Tumbling Dice' a track from the forthcoming Exile On Mainstreet album. It will reach No.5 in the British charts.

17 Apr Anita Pallenberg gives birth to a daughter, Dandelion, in Switzerland.

26 May Exile On Main Street, a double album, is released by Rolling Stones Records.

3 Jun The seventh North American tour opens in Vancouver. Thirty policemen are injured as 2,000 fans attempt to gatecrash.

31 Jul The marathon tour finishes in New York on Mick Jagger's birthday.

9 Aug Keith Richard, Anita and their children move to Montreux, Switzerland.

20 Nov Mick Jagger sings back-up on Carly Simon's single 'You're So Vain'.

25 Nov Band members convene in Kingston, Jamaica for four weeks' recording.

23 Dec An earthquake devastates Nicaragua. After Christmas Mick and Bianca Jagger fly there to search for her family and bring medicines. A benefit concert for victims of the earthquake will be announced in the new year. Various fund-raising activities eventually raise £350,000.

Keith arrested

Above: Keith pictured with his son Marlon. Keith and Anita also had a daughter, Angela (called Dandelion), born in Switzerland in May 1972. The couple were to suffer a personal tragedy in June 1976 when their third child Tara died of respiratory problems when he was only 10 weeks old.

Below: In June 1973 Keith and Anita were in a London court on drug charges. Keith was also charged with possession of a firearm and ammunition without a licence. They were released on £1,000 bail apiece.

Sell-out gigs

Left: Following performances in Vienna and West Germany in the autumn of 1973, the band returned for a series of concerts in the UK. Mick's aggressive posturing and the band's rebellious image continued to attract sell-out audiences for all the gigs.

Below: Keith accompanies Mick as the phenomenon of the Stones rolls on at Wembley. The rhythm guitarist was awaiting the resolution of his most recent court case. He was eventually fined £205 and given a conditional discharge when he attended Great Marlborough Street Magistrates' Court in October of the same year.

Exile on main street

Above: Mick lets rip in one of several tour dates in Wembley on the 1973 European tour and (left) demonstrates his agility at Wembley. He had been voted one of the 100 best dressed men in the world in a magazine poll in March 1970. During later tours Mick cultivated an overtly sexual image with his slinky, tight outfits and laced lycra jumpsuits, often displaying a wide expanse of smooth chest.

Mick Taylor had long been disenchanted with his position in the band and this led to his departure at the end of 1974, soon after the release the album *It's Only Rock 'n' Roll*.

1973 Timeline

4 Jan Confirmation of their safety in Managua averts fears that misadventure has befallen Mick and Bianca Jagger.

8 Jan Mick's hopes to play in Japan are dashed as an old drugs conviction prevents his entry. A tour has to be cancelled despite record-breaking ticket sales. Even so, three months later the band were voted group of the year and Jagger best vocalist in a Japanese magazine poll.

21/22 The Rolling Stones preview their Australasian tour with two concerts in Honolulu.

Mar The new album is mixed in Los Angeles.

11 Apr The School of Literature at California State University announces that it is to run degree courses in rock music. Amongst the performers whose work is to be studied are Mick Jagger and Keith Richard.

9 Jun Mick Jagger denies rumours that Keith is leaving the band. The denial is echoed by Keith two days later.

15 Jun Whilst mixing their new album, Goats Head Soup, at Island Studios in London, Keith Richard – now domiciled in Jamaica – speaks of plans to record with a rastafarian band.

18 Jun Marsha Hunt files an application at a London court, claiming Mick Jagger is her daughter Karis's father. The court orders that blood tests are taken.

26 Jun Keith Richard and two others are arrested in Chelsea for possession of cannabis. Keith is also charged with possessing a firearm and ammunition without a licence. He is remanded on bail.

26 Jul Mick Jagger is thirty. Plans are afoot for a new European tour to begin in September. Bianca will not travel with him. Mick denies their marriage is faltering.

31 Jul A fire causes serious damage to Keith and Anita's Sussex home.

6 Aug Tickets for the forthcoming UK tour go on sale and are an almost instant sell-out. Further venues and dates are arranged.

20 Aug 'Angie', recorded in Jamaica, is released and will chart at No.2. Both the single and the album it was cut from will be No. 1 in the USA in October.

31 Aug Goats Head Soup is released and will hold the No.1 position for two weeks.

1 Sept The European tour opens in Mannheim, West Germany.

7 Sept First British leg of the tour at Wembley – one of four dates there.

17 Sept Final British show in Birmingham. The tour continues with concerts in Germany, Holland, Belgium and Scandinavia, closing in Berlin on 19 October.

24 Oct Keith Richard is fined £205 for possession of various drugs, firearms and ammunition. For her possession of Mandrax, Anita Pallenberg is conditionally discharged.

13 Nov The Rolling Stones begin new recording sessions in Munich.

It's only rock 'n' roll

Below: Mick pictured in May 1974 wearing one of the rhinestone-studded jumpsuits he favoured at this time. Soon after this, the band released the lead single from the near-namesake parent album, *Its Only Rock 'n' Roll (But I Like It)*. Released in July 1974, the record reached number 16 in the States and number 10 in the UK singles chart – the lowest chart placing since their first chart successes in 1963.

Below right: The modest, rather introverted, bass guitarist Bill Wyman started his musical career playing the organ with his father and learnt to play the piano at the age of 10. When he later taught himself to play the bass guitar he decided this was definitely the instrument for him.

Right: A leather-clad Mick Jagger works the crowd at the Empire Pool, Wembley on 7 September 1973.

Ronnie replaces Mick Taylor

Ronnie Wood initially joined the Stones on a temporary basis in April 1975. Mick Taylor had long been disenchanted with his position in the band and felt that his contributions were not valued sufficiently. This led to his departure at the end of 1974, soon after the release of his last album with the group, *It's Only Rock 'n' Roll*.

The affable Ronnie Wood had begun his musical career with The Birds in 1964. When the group disbanded in 1967, he joined the Jeff Beck Group along with singer Rod Stewart. After several tours with them the pair then joined the Small Faces, soon to reform as the Faces, where Ronnie was known for his distinctive guitar work as well as co-writing many of their songs.

He had been on friendly terms with the Stones for some years and was initially asked to help out on their Tour of the Americas in June 1975. He was the perfect foil for the unreliable Keith Richard, who had constantly clashed with Mick Taylor. The Faces announced their break-up in December 1975, and Wood was officially pronounced a member of the Rolling Stones soon after.

Inset: Ronnie Wood pictured with his wife Krissie.

Tour of the Americas

Left: Mick pictured in 1975. The Stones' biggest ever tour, Tour of the Americas, started at Louisiana State University, Baton Rouge, on 1 June 1975. The band played a series of 58 concerts to 1.5 million people across North America, finishing in Buffalo, New York, on 8 August.

With so many concerts scheduled, the lead vocalist started to suffer with throat and larynx problems. Unusually, at a time when tours were considered a mechanism for promoting albums, the Tour of the Americas was not tied to the support of any newly released material. The band put out the compilation album, *Made in the Shade*, which only contained post-Decca compositions as the rights to their 1960s songs were owned by their former business manager Allen Klein.

Above: Mick and Bianca make a glamourous couple but rumours about an unhappy marriage persisted.

1974 Timeline

5 Jan Bill Wyman is in Los Angeles recording a solo album. Monkey Grip will be released in May on the Rolling Stones' own label.

10 Feb Mick Jagger once again denies that his marriage is on the rocks.

1 Mar A film about their US tour, Ladies and Gentlemen, The Rolling Stones is previewed in New York.

9 Jul The Rolling Stones preview 'It's Only Rock 'n' Roll (But I like It)' on BBC TV's Old Grey Whistle Test. The single hit the charts on 30 July, making No.10.

14 Jul Not for the first time, Keith Richard jams informally with Ronnie Wood at a north London venue.

27 Jul Mick answers a Brian Jones fan who expressed sorrow at the Stones apparent indifference to the anniversaries of Brian's death, explaining via a public letter that rather than send flowers to Brian's grave, band members sent donations to a United Nations children's charity that Brian had supported.

31 Aug Keith Richard cheerfully evades questions about his alleged complete blood transfusion in Switzerland.

7 Oct Mick is reported as saying he only married Bianca because she resembled him. Ten days later, in Paris, he is said to be dating Nathalie Delon.

7 Dec The band embark on a new recording in Munich.

12 Dec It is announced that Mick Taylor is leaving the band. In the first place he will work with former Cream bassist Jack Bruce. Massive speculation about his replacement centres on the possibility of Ronnie Wood of the Faces joining them.

31 Dec Ronnie Wood insists that his commitment remains with the Faces.

1975 Timeline

9 Feb After recording in Rotterdam Mick Jagger flies to New York whilst Keith Richard returns to London and works with Ronnie Wood at the latter's home studio in Richmond.

22 Mar Recording sessions continue in Munich where the band is soon joined by Ronnie Wood.

14 Apr It is announced that Ronnie Wood will join the Stones for part of their new American tour, but merely 'guesting' and on loan from the Faces.

1 May Central New York is brought to a stand-still as the Rolling Stones perform 'Brown Sugar' from the back of a truck. The tour as planned will be the band's longest ever.

13 May Ronnie Wood departs to join the Faces for their overlapping tour.

13 Jun Mid-tour the band release a compilation album, Made In The Shade, on their own label.

5 Jul Keith Richard, travelling with Ronnie Wood, is arrested on the highway in Fordyce, Arkansas, charged with possession of an offensive weapon – a tin-opener with a blade attachment. Both are released on bail.

More trouble with the law

Keith looks relaxed before a concert in Baton Rouge, Louisiana. However, the American tour was not all plain sailing for the lead guitarist as he was arrested in Arkansas on 5 July while travelling from Memphis to Dallas with fellow Stones member Ronnie Wood. Keith was charged with reckless driving and carrying a concealed weapon. The knife charge was later dropped and Richard was fined $162.50 after pleading guilty to the driving charge.

The 1975 Tour of the Americas was Ronnie Wood's first Rolling Stones tour, although he didn't officially join the band until December.

American tour

The grandiose American tour had been announced in typical ostentatious fashion when the band performed "Brown Sugar" while driving down New York's Fifth Avenue on the back of a flatbed truck. Their flamboyant tactics continued when the concerts started and included extravagant, outrageous props and a stage designed as a lotus plant which opened at the beginning of the shows to reveal the band inside and the giant inflatable phallus (left). The tour was originally planned to cover South America as well as the northern continent, but a combination of currency fluctuations and concerns over security meant that concerts scheduled for Mexico, Brazil and Venezuela were cancelled.

Above: Mick and Keith share the microphone.

Tour of Europe '76

Opposite: Following the Tour of the Americas, the band continued their punishing schedule with the Tour of Europe '76 which started in April. Mick gives an electrifying performance on stage at Earls Court. The Stones' shows always delivered an elaborate spectacle to their mesmerised audiences, helped by the use of an eclectic range of props varying from a suspended 80-foot silk dragon to clowns, confetti and even cannon fire. It was after one of the concerts at this venue that Keith learned that his 10-week-old baby son Tara had died. Despite being devastated by the tragedy, Keith insisted that the tour continue.

Below: Ronnie, Mick and Keith pictured with Ollie Brown and Billy Preston. "Fool to Cry", the lead single from the album *Black and Blue*, featured in the set list for the European tour. Another Jagger-Richards composition, the ballad became a worldwide hit, although it only reached number 6 in the UK singles chart. It has been reported that Keith Richards was in such a bad state during the the tour that he fell asleep on stage while playing this song in Germany!

Right: Mick and Ronnie on stage in London.

1976 Timeline

26 Feb Release of Stone Alone, Bill Wyman's solo album.

28 Feb It is unofficially announced that Ronnie Wood will join the band.

26 Mar Anita gives birth to a second son, Tara, in Switzerland.

10 Apr Rehearsals for a new European tour begin in France.

20 Apr Release of the album Black And Blue. It enters the British charts a week later and reaches No. 2.

28 Apr The tour opens in Frankfurt.

8 May 'Fool To Cry' enters the British singles charts. It will reach No.4.

10 May The British tour begins with a show in Glasgow.

19 May After crashing his Bentley in Buckinghamshire Keith, Anita and Marlon are unhurt but the car is a write-off. Police find 'substances' in the wreckage and he is arrested but released as the substances must be identified before any charge is brought. Richard was astonished to learn later that the substances were LSD and cocaine and some newspapers speculated that a Rolling Stone could be used as an unwitting drugs courier.

4 Jun Just before going onstage at the Abattoirs for the first of three concerts in Paris, Keith Richard learns that his ten-week-old son Tara has died of a mysterious virus. White and stricken he played on, and insisted that the tragedy should remain secret and that tour plans should not be disrupted.

11 Jun The Rolling Stones play in Barcelona – their first Spanish concert. Ten days later they give their first show in Yugoslavia.

21 Aug The band performs before 200,000 fans, headlining the Knebworth Festival.

New rumours of tension in the Jagger marriage circulate when they go their separate ways after Mick meets Bianca at Heathrow airport.

20 Sept Mick Jagger attends a London Sex Pistols gig at a club. This month he and Ronnie Wood have whittled down 150 hours of live concert tapes for a new live LP.

6 Oct Before a magistrate Keith Richard chooses to go to a higher court for his recent charges to be heard. Bail is renewed at £5,000.

30 Oct Krissie Wood gives birth to a son, Jesse James.

Right and overleaf: The Rolling Stones headlining the Knebworth Festival on 21 August 1976.

The Stones played to an estimated audience of 200,000 at Knebworth, their first pop festival since the disaster at Altamont.

Back in court

Above left and middle: Yet another drug-related court appearance for Keith Richard in January 1977. The white-faced Stone had been arrested in May 1976 after he crashed his Bentley on the M1 near Newport Pagnell and police found LSD and cocaine in the wreckage. Anita and son Marlon had been in the car when the accident happened, but were unhurt despite the fact that the car was written off.

Above right: Bill and Astrid lead a quieter life.

Left: Mick flew in from Los Angeles to attend the court hearing at Aylesbury Crown Court in Buckinghamshire and offer support to his long-time friend. The apprehensive-looking lead guitarist had pleaded not guilty to all the charges. Mick sat in the public gallery throughout the three-day trial and watched intently as Keith took the witness stand.

Below: Ronnie Wood relaxes at his Richmond home early in 1976. Ronnie is a talented artist as well as a musician. His two brothers also demonstrated both artistic and musical talents; his older brother Art was lead singer in a sixties R & B group, The Artwoods.

Keith faces serious charges

Middle left: Smiles all around as a very relieved Keith celebrates with Mick after being found not guilty of possessing LSD, but guilty of possession of cocaine and fined £750 plus costs in Aylesbury. However, he was soon to be in trouble again as he and Anita travelled to Toronto in February. Anita was arrested at the airport when a quantity of drugs was found in her luggage. A few days later, the Royal Canadian Mounted Police raided Keith's hotel room where they found the comatose Stone plus enough drugs to charge him with the extremely serious charge of drug trafficking – a crime that carried a maximum life sentence.

Below: The Stones minus Keith (who was unable to attend the launch party at The Marquee as he was undergoing drug rehabilitation therapy in the States after his arrest in Toronto) attend the launch of the new album *Love You Live* at London's Marquee Club in the summer of 1977. The double live album was drawn from Tour of the Americas in 1975, the European Tour in 1976 and club shows from Toronto in 1977. Keith lived under threat of criminal prosecution until the case finally came to court in October 1978 when he was given a year's suspended sentence and ordered to give a charity concert the following year.

Above left: Mick attends a ball to celebrate the Queen's Silver Jubilee in July 1977.

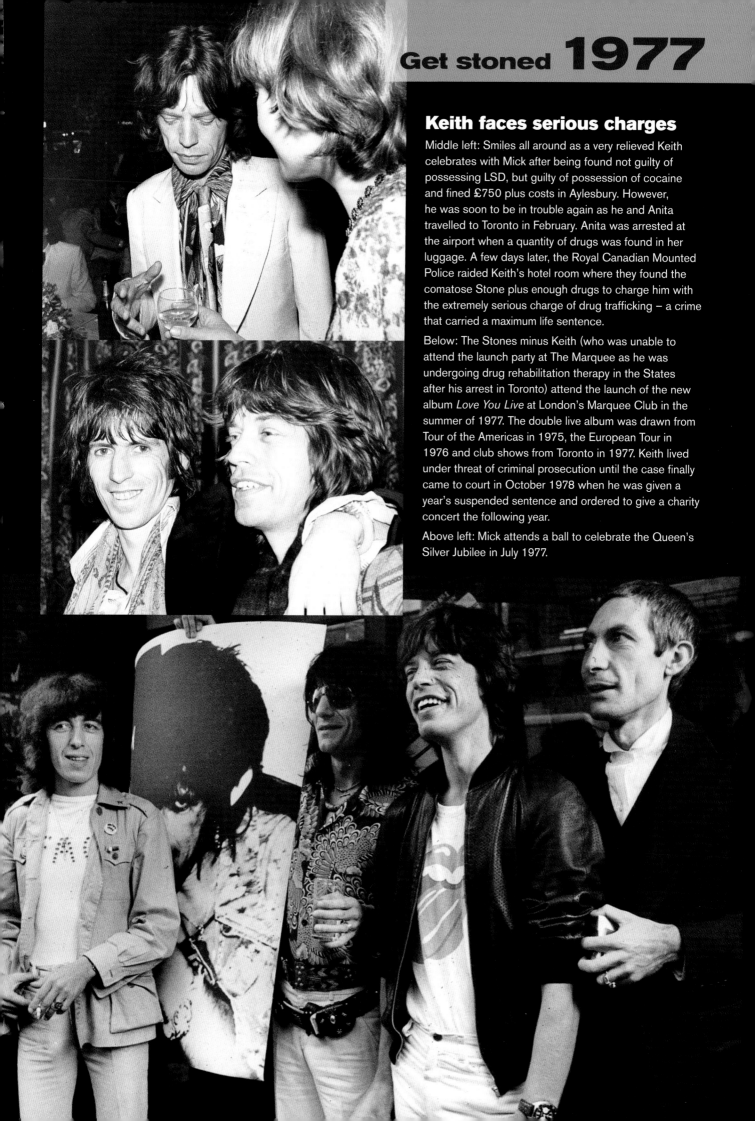

1977 Timeline

12 Jan At Aylesbury Crown Court, after a three day trial with Mick lending supportive presence, Keith is found guilty of possessing cocaine.

Feb The first of Keith and Anita's next slew of drug-related travails takes place at Toronto airport, on the way to a short but troubled new tour. Their luggage is searched and Anita is arrested, then released. Days later both are charged with possession of heroin but released, Keith on bail. A court hearing is eventually set for March 14 when Anita is fined $400. For his alleged crimes Keith is remanded on bail.

4 Mar Margaret Trudeau, glamorous wife of Canada's Premier Pierre Trudeau, throws a party for the band after their opening gig at a small club. As the tour progresses and she parties with them elsewhere, both she and members of the Rolling Stones dismiss rumours of inappropriate behaviour as mischievous gossip. Mrs Trudeau's husband is staunchly supportive of her.

15 May Touring in Britain Nils Lofgren dedicates his song 'Keith Don't Go (To Toronto)' to Richard whose voluntary treatment for drug addiction renders him unable to attend a Toronto court appearance. It is rescheduled for 19 July when he is once again unable to appear. The case is adjourned to December. Meanwhile German fans raised a collection to help with his fees and plan a demonstration outside their Canadian embassy in support of Keith.

13 Sept The live album which will reach No.3 in the British charts, Love You Live is launched at the Marquee Club in London.

23 Sept The film of the band in concert, Ladies And Gentlemen, The Rolling Stones is premiered at the Rainbow Theatre in London.

2 Dec Appearing at a Toronto court Keith Richard hears that his trial is postponed. Further delays mean that he will have to wait until October 1978.

11 Dec As Bianca Jagger leaves London, rumours of a divorce become louder.

1978

27 Jan Charlie Watts plays with a skiffle group in Swindon.

19 Mar Krissie Wood files for divorce, citing model Jo Howard in her petition.

14 May Bianca Jagger files for divorce in London.

19 May 'Miss You' is released. It reaches No.2 in the British charts.

9 Jun The Some Girls album is released the day before their American tour opens in Florida. 55,000 tickets for the 10 July gig at Anaheim, California sell out within two hours. More than $1,000,000 is taken in advance sales for the 80,000 capacity auditorium in New Orleans where the band play on 13 July.

26 Jul The tour ends at Oakland, California, on Mick Jagger's thirty-fifth birthday.

20 Oct As of now, Keith is once again Keith Richards.

23 Oct Keith Richards' trial in Toronto starts at last. He is given a one year suspended prison sentence and ordered to give a charity concert. People incensed by the judge's leniency will begin an appeal for a harsher sentence the following month.

3 Dec Keith's first solo single, 'Run Rudolph Run' is released in the USA. The UK release in February misses the Christmas rush.

15 Dec Japan relents after six years and lifts its ban on the Rolling Stones.

28 Dec The band are voted artists of the year and Some Girls album of the year in a Rolling Stone magazine poll.

1979

21 Apr The Rolling Stones give their only live performance of the year in Toronto, arranged by Keith Richards to meet his recent sentencing stipulation.

18 Jun The band gathers in Paris to cut a new album. Work will continue intermittently for some months.

18 Dec At his birthday party in New York Keith Richards meets American model Patti Hansen, whom he will eventually marry.

1980

18 Feb Bill Wyman tells the Daily Express that he plans to leave the band in two years' time – their twentieth anniversary.

20 Jun The single 'Emotional Rescue', taken from the forthcoming album of the same name, is released. It will reach No. 1 and stay there for four weeks. The next single, 'She's So Cold' is released in September but is less successful.

11 Oct Recording sessions for a new album begin in Paris.

1981

4 Mar The anthology LP, Sucking In The Seventies is produced by Mick and Keith and released on the Rolling Stones' label. It will have mixed fortunes, many American shops refusing to stock it because of the title, and only charts for a few weeks, peaking at No. 17. It will be released in the UK on 13 April.

Jul Wyman's 'Je Suis Un Rock Star' is released and reaches No.11 in the British charts.

14 Aug Rehearsals for a new tour begin in Massachusetts.

17 Aug 'Start Me Up', produced by Mick and Keith, is released, taken from the forthcoming Tattoo You album. It will sell a million copies in the US in the week of its early September release.

25 Sept The tour opens in Philadelphia before a 90,000 strong crowd.

19 Dec Another tour finishes in Virginia. It is estimated that the band grossed $50 million in ticket sales and earned almost half as much again via merchandising, record sales and sponsorship. A film of the fifty-date tour has been shot by Hal Ashby for release in 1982.

Charlie flies solo

Right: The lugubrious Charlie Watts is at his most relaxed when doing what comes naturally. He has always been a huge fan of jazz and in 1964 he published an illustrated book about the legendary Charlie Parker entitled *Ode to a High Flying Bird*. In the late 1970s he joined Stones founding member Ian Stewart and Bob Hall in the boogie-woogie band, Rocket 88 which then released a live record of a concert in Germany.

For the Stones, the release of the album *Some Girls* in 1978 revitalised their career. The LP incorporated the punk influences that were so significant at the time and became their biggest-selling album to date. It was the first album in 15 years on which Keith added the "s" back to his surname (making him "Richards") since Andrew Oldham had suggested he drop it in 1963.

Mick's new love

Above: Mick with his new belle, the leggy Texan model Jerry Hall. The couple had first met when she was with Bryan Ferry, lead singer of Roxy Music. Jerry Hall's modelling career began in France in the early 1970s and her trademark long blond hair and commanding height soon ensured she was one of the most photographed models of the time.

Left: Mick sports a shorter hairstyle on stage at Shea Stadium, New York, during the 1981 American Tour. The three-month tour covered cities across the length and breadth of the States. In fact it was impossible to keep up with demand for tickets and many additional concerts were added to the original schedule.

Adventurous stage sets, supported by vibrant props, were particularly suited to the outdoor concerts which mainly took place in the daytime.

September 1981: US tour kicks off in Philadelphia

The tour kicked off at the JFK Stadium in Philadelphia on 25 September 1981. Mick used all his experience to whip up the enormous crowd on a very hot day.

The tour was used as a means of promoting the band's latest album, *Tattoo You,* which had followed swiftly on the heels of *Emotional Rescue. Tattoo You* was an eclectic LP but contained little in the way of new material, consisting mainly of an assembly of ideas stretching back to *Goats Head Soup.* However, it proved to be a big commercial success and reached number 1 in the US album charts. The album had been recorded among growing tensions and differences in personal ambitions within the band – particularly between Mick Jagger and Keith Richards. Although it was a commercial success it was was panned by the critics.

The band had released their latest single "Start Me Up" shortly before the beginning of the American tour. It was originally recorded with a reggae beat and was the opening song on the *Tattoo You* album. With its infectious riff, the single sold over a million copies in the first week of its release and is still often used as an opening song in Stones' live shows.

Fifty-million-dollar tour

Mick with Ronnie in the background. The American tour was estimated to have grossed $50 million in ticket sales with further income from merchandise. The group had also secured an innovative sponsorship deal with the Jovan perfume company who paid to have their name on the Rolling Stones tickets. The lucrative US tour also raised money through the sale of TV and movie rights. In another first, the band's performance at the Hampton Coliseum, Virginia, in December was broadcast on pay-per-view and in closed circuit cinemas and Hollywood director Hal Ashby, a Rolling Stones fan, accompanied the group on the tour, filming the documentary *Let's Spend the Night Together* which was eventually shown on cable TV.

Opposite: Mick dons his bright puffer jacket before later stripping it off in the Philadelphia concert.

Opposite inset: Mick sings "Jumping Jack Flash" suspended above the crowd JFK stadium, Philadelphia.

Inset above: Thirty-eight-year-old Mick is in full swing in front of the oldest band member Bill Wyman, who celebrated his 45th birthday with a party at Disneyworld in Florida while in the States.

Back on stage in Europe

Right: The tumultuous trio of Ronnie, Keith and Mick perform at Wembley in June 1982 in their first European tour for six years. When performing Mick usually favoured bright primary colours for his unique costumes while Keith and Ronnie tended towards the more orthodox rock 'n' roll outfit of worn jeans and waistcoat.

The Stones had released their live album, *Still Life (American Concert 1981)*, to coincide with their European Tour. The LP had been recorded during the 1981 American tour and was widely denounced for being too slick, with none of the rough edges usually associated with the band. Nevertheless it was yet another success on both sides of the Atlantic.

Below: Prior to the European tour the band managed to arrange an unpublicised show at the intimate 100 Club at 100 Oxford Street in London. The club is one of the most famous live venues in Europe and has been host to a diverse repertoire of acts since it opened in 1942.

The 1982 Europe tour comprised 36 dates, beginning in Scotland and ending in Leeds, and was to be the Stones' last tour for seven years.

Triumphant tour

Opposite, above and right: The triumphant tour closed in front of around 80,000 fans at Roundhay Park in Leeds on 25 July, the night before Mick's 39th birthday. The previous evening the band had played to another huge crowd at the stunning Slane Castle, Ireland, on a picturesque site near the River Boyne.

As the tour came to an end the band's thoughts turned to future projects and a few months later work started on what was to be the next Stones LP, *Undercover*. The hard-rock album consisted of all newly recorded material and was released in November 1983. This was a time when the feuding between the Glimmer Twins was increasing and the friction between them led to further deterioration within their relationship and disillusionment among the other band members.

Solo album for Mick

Above: Ronnie and Charlie smile cheerfully for the camera but both Keith and Mick are more reserved.

Left: Mick has a twinkle in his eye at the christening of daughter, Elizabeth Scarlett in 1984. Mick released his debut solo album, *She's the Boss*, in February 1985. This caused further antagonism within the band as they were simultaneously trying to put together The Stones' next album, *Dirty Work*. The other members resented the fact that Mick was putting all his efforts into material for his solo work and not giving enough attention to their joint undertaking.

July 1984 would see the release of the album, *Rewind (1971–1984)* – a retrospective of the previous 13 years. The UK and US editions of the album featured different track listings, reflecting the individual tastes of the two markets.

Left: Elegantly attired, as ever, Charlie is pictured in October 1984. He had been involved in several jazz-oriented albums and steadfastly pursued his passion for jazz, taking every opportunity to play in a variety of settings.

Far left: After his split from Anita Pallenberg, Keith embarked on a steady relationship with American model Patti Hansen. He had met her at his birthday party in 1979 and they soon became an item. They married on 18 December 1983, Keith's 40th birthday. They have two daughters, Theodora and Alexandra.

Timeline 1982

11 Jan 'Hang Fire' is released in the US.

4 Mar The Rolling Stones collect a slew of awards in Rolling Stone magazine's annual prize-giving. They are voted band of the year and Jagger best vocalist. Tattoo You is judged best album and 'Start Me Up' best single. Jagger and Richards are best songwriters and Keith is best instrumentalist. Later this month Jagger and Richards start editing Hal Ashby's tapes of the recent US tour.

26 Apr The band's first UK concert for 6 years – in Aberdeen. European dates in England, Ireland, France, Spain, Holland, Germany, Austria, Belgium, Sweden, Switzerland, Denmark and Italy are arranged.

Jun Sell-out concerts in London and Bristol. The tour finishes at Leeds.

1 Jun A live album, Still Life, is released.

24 Jun On behalf of the band Bill Wyman collects the British Music Industry's award for outstanding achievement. Keith Richards is interviewed for BBC 2's Newsnight

7 Nov Recording sessions resume at the Paris studios.

12 Nov Keith Richards confirms reports in the Sun that he and Patti Hansen are to marry. Jerry Hall flies from New York to Paris. The following day Venezuelan model Victoria Vicuna joins Mick in Paris. A double anthology album, The Best Of The Rolling Stones, is released this month on a budget label.

1983

14 Jan Mick Jagger plays the Chinese Emperor in a US TV production of The Nightingale by Hans Christian Andersen.

25 Jan In a Sun interview Mick Jagger talks about the possibility of the Stones breaking up. He tells John Blake that it will disintegrate very slowly and that he doesn't know what goals are left.

25 Apr To celebrate the 25th anniversary of the Marquee in London, Charlie Watts and Bill Wyman join Alexis Korner on stage.

4 Jul Mick Jagger tells the Daily Star how he has moderated his earlier drink and drugs lifestyle now that he has to retain peak fitness for touring demands. He will turn forty on 26 July.

25 Aug The Rolling Stones sign with CBS in a $28 million deal said to make music business history. Later in August it is announced that Jerry Hall is pregnant and that Bill Wyman is splitting from Astrid Lindstrum, his girlfriend for fourteen years.

20 Sept At a Royal Albert Hall concert in London, fundraising for ARMS, the multiple sclerosis charity, Charlie Watts, Eric Clapton, Steve Winwood, Jeff Beck and Jimmy Page join MS sufferer Ronnie Lane on stage. Ten months later a live album, The Ronnie Lane Appeal to ARMS, is released.

30 Oct 'Undercover Of The Night' is released. A week later the album, Undercover, is released on Rolling Stones Records. Three days later the BBC bans the video and the next day Mick Jagger defends it on a Channel 4 youth programme, The Tube. The single will reach No.12 in the British charts and the album Undercover No.1.

9 Dec Final date of a short US tour to raise cash for ARMS, in New York.

18 Dec On his fortieth birthday Keith Richards marries Patti Hansen in Mexico.

1984

23 Jan New single 'She Was Hot' is released. It dips into the UK charts at No. 40 and only makes No. 44 in the US listings, possibly hindered by the banning of a raunchy video which featured the trouser flies of band members popping open.

2 Mar A daughter, Elizabeth Scarlett, is born to Jerry Hall and Mick Jagger in New York.

27 Mar Critical remarks made by Bill Wyman about band members are published in the Sun. A week later he denies having made them.

6 May Mick Jagger begins working on a song, 'State Of Shock', with Michael Jackson in New York. It is released in June, reaching No. 3 in the US charts and No. 14 in Britain in July.

29 Jun Rewind, a compilation LP, is released and reaches No.12 in the UK charts.

Sept Tour plans are postponed because of Mick Jagger's solo schedules. Bill Wyman produces an LP by Willie and the Poor Boys, featuring Charlie Watts and other musicians.

Nov Band members meet in Amsterdam to discuss their future. Mick, Jerry and film/video producer Julian Temple fly to Rio de Janeiro to shoot a promo video for Jagger's new album.

1985

4 Feb Mick Jagger's first solo single, 'Just Another Night', is released in the UK and US. It is taken from his forthcoming album, She's The Boss and will reach No.27 in the UK singles charts.

13 Jul The Live Aid concerts take place in London and Philadelphia, broadcast to a global audience of 1.6 billion. The Rolling Stones as such do not take part but Mick, Keith and Ronnie all separately play their parts.

23 Aug The single of Mick duetting with David Bowie on 'Dancing In The Street' is released w and becomes a disco classic, thanks partly to an inspired video. It is immediately No. 1 in the UK charts.

28 Aug James Leroy Augustine is born to Mick Jagger and Jerry Hall in New York.

18 Nov Charlie Watts, who has been developing his early jazz interest, opens for a week at Ronnie Scott's club in London with his 29-piece Big Band. Jack Bruce and Stan Tracey are amongst the musicians. Performances are attended by Keith, Mick and Bill.

25 Nov Work on the new album resumes in New York. A few days later Mick Jagger sings 'Honky Tonk Women' with Tina Turner in Carolina.

12 Dec Ian Stewart, friend, colleague, some-time back-up musician and management stalwart dies of a heart attack in London, aged 47. His funeral on 20 December is attended by all the Rolling Stones. On 23 February 1986 the band played at an invitation-only memorial gig for Ian Stewart at the 100 Club in London.

Live Aid

Above: Mick and Jerry with David Bowie. Jagger and Bowie were soon to collaborate on the single "Dancing in the Street" as part of the Live Aid charity event. The original plan was to play the song live in two cities, with Bowie performing in London while Jagger simultaneously sang in Philadelphia. However, the satellite link would have meant there was a time difference of about half a second. Another solution was needed and the pair eventually shot a video together which was shown at both venues during the Live Aid concert in July 1985. When the single was released in August it shot straight to number 1 in the UK charts. Reflecting the fractured state of the band at the time, the five Stones did not play together at the Live Aid concert. Mick performed a solo, backed by Hall and Oates and also appeared with Tina Turner, while Keith and Ronnie played with Bob Dylan.

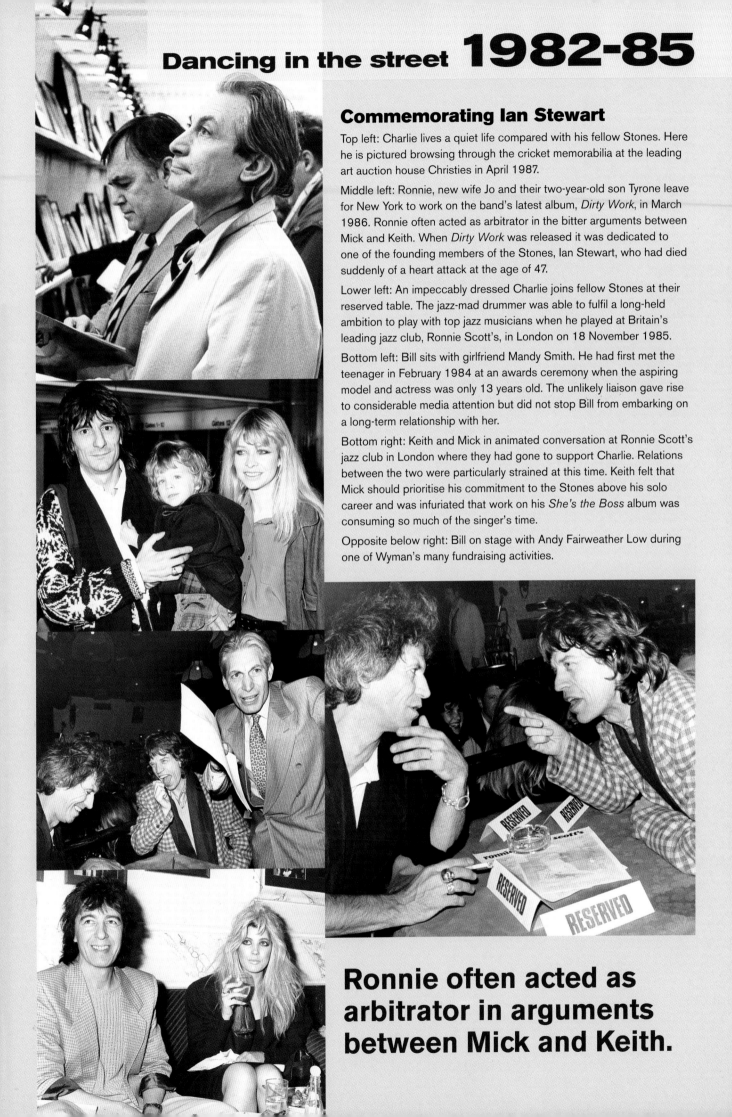

Commemorating Ian Stewart

Top left: Charlie lives a quiet life compared with his fellow Stones. Here he is pictured browsing through the cricket memorabilia at the leading art auction house Christies in April 1987.

Middle left: Ronnie, new wife Jo and their two-year-old son Tyrone leave for New York to work on the band's latest album, *Dirty Work*, in March 1986. Ronnie often acted as arbitrator in the bitter arguments between Mick and Keith. When *Dirty Work* was released it was dedicated to one of the founding members of the Stones, Ian Stewart, who had died suddenly of a heart attack at the age of 47.

Lower left: An impeccably dressed Charlie joins fellow Stones at their reserved table. The jazz-mad drummer was able to fulfil a long-held ambition to play with top jazz musicians when he played at Britain's leading jazz club, Ronnie Scott's, in London on 18 November 1985.

Bottom left: Bill sits with girlfriend Mandy Smith. He had first met the teenager in February 1984 at an awards ceremony when the aspiring model and actress was only 13 years old. The unlikely liaison gave rise to considerable media attention but did not stop Bill from embarking on a long-term relationship with her.

Bottom right: Keith and Mick in animated conversation at Ronnie Scott's jazz club in London where they had gone to support Charlie. Relations between the two were particularly strained at this time. Keith felt that Mick should prioritise his commitment to the Stones above his solo career and was infuriated that work on his *She's the Boss* album was consuming so much of the singer's time.

Opposite below right: Bill on stage with Andy Fairweather Low during one of Wyman's many fundraising activities.

Ronnie often acted as arbitrator in arguments between Mick and Keith.

"Let's Work"

Below and opposite: The lead single "Let's Work" from parent album *Primitive Cool* was released prior to the LP, hitting the shops in September 1987. Mick made a live appearance on BBC's *Top of the Pops* on 24 September to promote the song, but it was only a minor hit.

Right: Bill takes American model Nike Clark to Langan's Brasserie before the couple go on to the exclusive Tramp nightclub early in 1987. His relationship with Mandy Smith had been waning since August 1986. However, it was not the end of the road as their affair was later re-kindled and the couple would marry in 1989.

Primitive Cool

Below: Jerry and Mick relax on the beach in Barbados in January 1987 shortly before he began work on his second solo album *Primitive Cool*. Relations between Mick and Keith had soured further when Mick decided his project would take precedence over any Stones commitments. The album was a more reflective piece of work than his debut offering, *She's the Boss*, and was co-produced by Eurythmics guitarist Dave Stewart. While Mick was busy compiling his solo album, Keith was involved in a documentary about Chuck Berry in honour of Berry's 60th birthday. The film *Hail! Hail! Rock 'n' Roll* chronicled two special performances from the pioneer of the musical genre that so influenced the lead guitarist. Keith also formed a band named the X-Pensive Winos with American songwriter and producer, Steve Jordan. Keith released his own solo album, *Talk is Cheap*, in October 1988 and received some warm reviews. This album also spawned a brief US tour – only one of two that Keith has done as a solo artist.

Timeline 1986

25 Feb The Rolling Stones are given a Lifetime Achievement Award at the Grammies in Los Angeles, presented to them by Eric Clapton.

3 Mar Latest single 'Harlem Shuffle' is released. It will reach No. 7 in the UK charts and No.5 in the USA.

24 Mar The new album, Dirty Work is released. It enters the British charts in April and will reach No.3.

19 Apr The Charlie Watts Orchestra begins a week's engagement at Ronnie Scott's club.

20 Jun Before the Prince and Princess of Wales, Mick Jagger – along with David Bowie, Elton John, Paul McCartney, Phil Collins, Eric Clapton and Tina Turner – takes part in a fundraiser for the Prince's Trust. Earlier in the month Ronnie Wood, and Keith Richards have been busy with separate musical commitments in the USA.

5 Jul Ronnie Wood and Bill Wyman join Rod Stewart on stage for a Faces reunion concert at Wembley.

12 Jul Keith discusses a possible film project with Chuck Berry in St Louis.

15 Jul Keith Richards joins Bob Dylan for concerts at Madison Square Garden, New York.

31 Jul Mick Jagger's single 'Ruthless People', theme song for a Disney film of the same name, is released. It has modest chart success.

26 Jul Patti Richards' daughter, Alexandra Nicole, is born in New York.

3 Aug Sixteen-year-old Mandy Smith speaks to a British newspaper about her relationship with Bill Wyman. It has lasted for over two years and now she is tiring of it.

29 Aug A version of 'Jumpin' Jack Flash', recorded by Aretha Franklin and produced by Ronnie and Keith, is released. It will reach No. 21 in the US charts in September.

15 Sept Mick discusses plans for his next album with Dave Stewart of the Eurythmics, in Los Angeles. Recording for the album will begin in Holland in November.

Nov Charlie Watts and his 33-piece orchestra arrive in New York for a short East Coast tour.

1987

13 Jun Charlie Watts and his orchestra play at the Playboy Jazz Festival in Hollywood.

13 Jul Keith discusses a Virgin solo deal with Richard Branson. It is signed on 17 July.

31 Aug Mick Jagger's single 'Let's Work' is released, reaching No.35 in UK.

14 Sept Mick Jagger's album, Primitive Cool, is released. It will reach No.18 in the British charts.

4 Nov Ronnie Wood opens a North American tour in Columbus, Ohio.

19 Dec Ronnie Wood and Bo Diddley play at the opening of Woody's On The Beach in Miami.

1988

20 Jan At the annual Rock 'n' Roll Hall of Fame in New York, Mick Jagger jams with Bruce Springsteen and George Harrison, and also with both Bob Dylan and Jeff Beck. He sings 'Satisfaction' solo.

20 Feb Bill Wyman and Ronnie Wood join Phil Collins, Eddy Grant, Ian Dury, Kenney Jones, Elvis Costello and Chris Rea at a Royal Albert Hall benefit that Bill has arranged for the Great Ormond Street Children's Hospital.

12 Mar Mick Jagger and Ronnie Wood meet at the former's hotel in Osaka. Both are in Japan on separate tours. Mick is reputed to receive £1,000,000 for each of his sell-out shows.

25 Mar By the time the Jagger tour closes in Nagoya, over a quarter of a million tickets have been sold. Before leaving Japan he guests with Tina Turner at her own concert in Osaka.

18 May All five members of the Rolling Stones meet for the first time in two years, at a London hotel. Plans for working together again and touring are discussed.

26 Jul Mick Jagger celebrates his 45th birthday and Jerry's first night in Bus Stop at a theatre in New Jersey. They dine after the show.

22 Aug Mick Jagger announces the Stones will record and tour together the following year. 'Satisfaction' is voted best single of the last 25 years by Rolling Stone magazine.

4 Oct Virgin release Talk Is Cheap, Keith Richards' first solo album.

16 Oct Keith Richards, whose own home has been damaged in the recent hurricane, plays at the fundraising Smile Jamaica concert in London.

24 Nov Keith Richards and his band the X-Pensive Winos open their US tour in Atlanta.

Bill weds Mandy

Above: Actress Barbara Bach, Ringo Starr's wife, poses with Mandy Smith, Bill Wyman and Jo and Ronnie Wood in May 1989 at the opening of Bill's latest venture – his rock 'n' roll themed restaurant, Sticky Fingers. By this time the rift between Mick and Keith had been healed after the pair had flown to Barbados in January to discuss the future of the band.

Below left: Bill kisses the cheek of his new bride, Mandy Smith, after the blessing at St John the Evangelist church in London in June 1989. The couple had been married officially in a secret civil ceremony at Bury St Edmunds a few days earlier. The three bridesmaids and page were all cousins of 18-year-old Amanda Louise Wyman, nee Smith. There was a party for more than 500 guests following the ceremony.

Below right: A few days after their marriage the happy couple enjoy a drink outside Bill's Sticky Fingers restaurant. Their marriage was to be short-lived and the unlikely pair were divorced two years later.

Timeline 1989

18 Jan   At the New York Hall of Fame awards the band is inducted.

15 Mar   The band sign a multi-million dollar contract – the biggest in rock and roll history – relating to promotion and merchandising of their next tour, for which over fifty dates are proposed.

9 May   Party to launch the opening of Bill Wyman's restaurant, Sticky Fingers, in Kensington. Montserrat recordings completed, this month sees the mixing of the new album in London.

2 Jun   Bill Wyman marries Mandy Smith quietly in Bury St Edmunds. Three days later the marriage is blessed in London and a reception is held at the Grosvenor House Hotel. Mick Jagger gives the couple a £200,000 Picasso etching.

11 Jul   The Stones announce the Steel Wheels tour at a press conference at Grand Central Station, New York. There will be an album of the same name. Advance ticket sales for the tour break all records. The band and their entourage set up elaborate camp in Washington, Connecticut.

17 Aug   A new single, 'Mixed Emotions', is released. It reaches No.5 in the US.

31 Aug   Tour opens in Philadelphia. Black market tickets sell for up to forty times the original price.

9 Sept   'Mixed Emotions' enters the British charts, reaching No.33.

19 Dec   Last date of the North American tour, in Atlantic City.

1990

Feb   The Stones tour Japan for the first time.

14 Feb   First of the Steel Wheels dates in Tokyo.

8 Mar   Rolling Stone magazine nominates the Stones as best band and artists of the year for 1989, Steel Wheels best album and 'Mixed Emotions' best single. Mick is nominated best male singer, Bill best bassist and Charlie best drummer.

22 Mar   Mick announces the Urban Jungle European tour in London. It will feature a new stage set and lighting and a different playing order from the Steel Wheels shows. By the following day 120,000 tickets for the Wembley concerts have sold out.

18 May   The tour opens in Rotterdam and moves on through France, Germany, Portugal, Spain, Ireland, Italy, Austria, Sweden, Norway and Denmark.

Jul   Release of Voodoo Lounge album.

4 Jul   British concerts (between shows in Paris and Dublin), open with several at Wembley and one in Glasgow.

9 Aug   European leg of the tour closes in Copenhagen.

Sep/Oct The tour continues in Australia.

Right: Keith and 19-year-old son Marlon at the Hard Rock Cafe in London in June 1989. Marlon, who had been named after the actor Marlon Brando, grew up in the States where he attended a Quaker school. He married model Lucie de la Falaise in Italy in 1994 and the couple have three children.

1991

1 Mar   Julian Temple directs the Highwire video in New York.

2 Apr   The Stone's fifth live album, Flashpoint, is released.

2 May   The Rolling Stones are honoured at the Ivor Novello Awards in London for their outstanding contribution to British music.

19 Nov   The Rolling Stones sign to Virgin Records.

10 Dec   Keith Richards and the X-Pensive Winos' live album is released on CD and video.

1992

Aug   Ronnie Wood's solo album, Slide On This, is released.

20 Oct   Keith Richards' second solo album, Main Offender, is released by Virgin.

27 Nov   Keith and the Winos begin a short European tour.

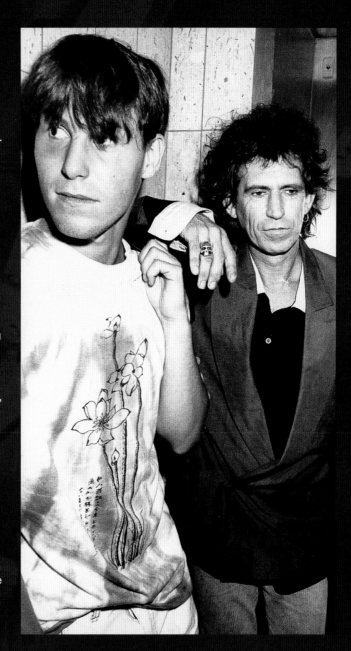

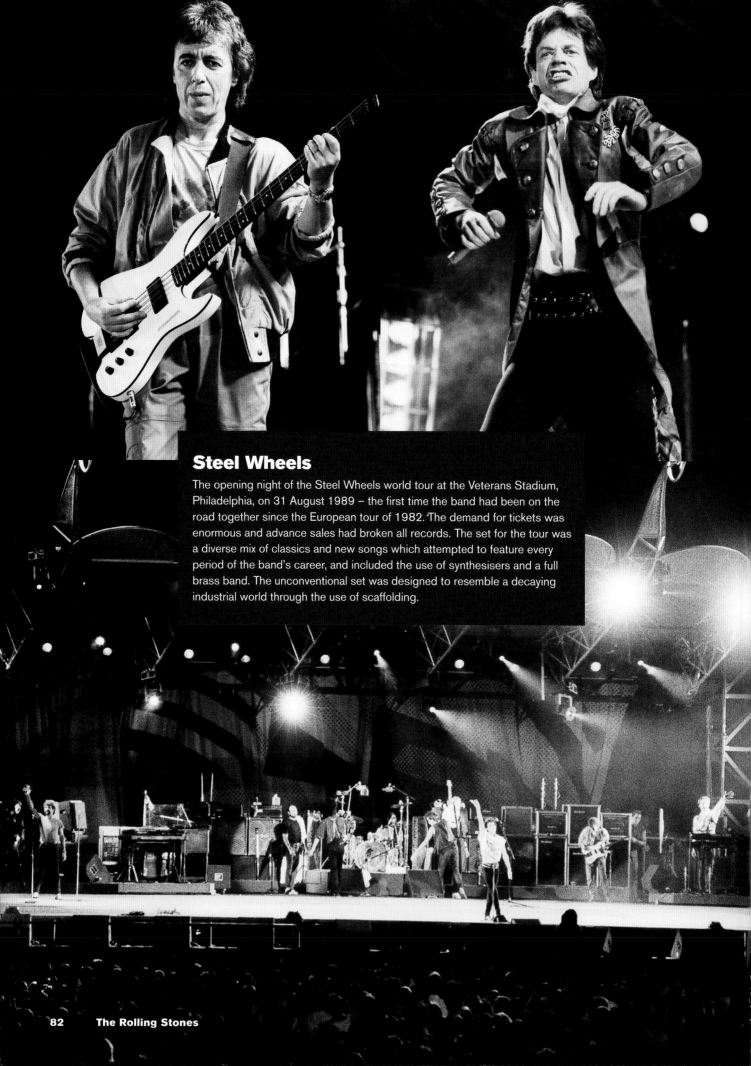

Steel Wheels

The opening night of the Steel Wheels world tour at the Veterans Stadium, Philadelphia, on 31 August 1989 – the first time the band had been on the road together since the European tour of 1982. The demand for tickets was enormous and advance sales had broken all records. The set for the tour was a diverse mix of classics and new songs which attempted to feature every period of the band's career, and included the use of synthesisers and a full brass band. The unconventional set was designed to resemble a decaying industrial world through the use of scaffolding.

Steel Wheels, recorded at the Air Studios at Monserrat, was Bill Wyman's final studio album with the band and the first not to feature any contribution from Ian Stewart, who had died in 1985.

"Mixed Emotions"

"Mixed Emotions", the single released from the tour album *Steel Wheels*, was a Jagger-Richards collaboration written during their time in Barbados in January 1989. The lyrics reflected much of the resentment and bitterness that had so dominated their relationship during the 1980s. The song only reached number 35 in the UK charts but fared better in the US where it peaked at number 5.

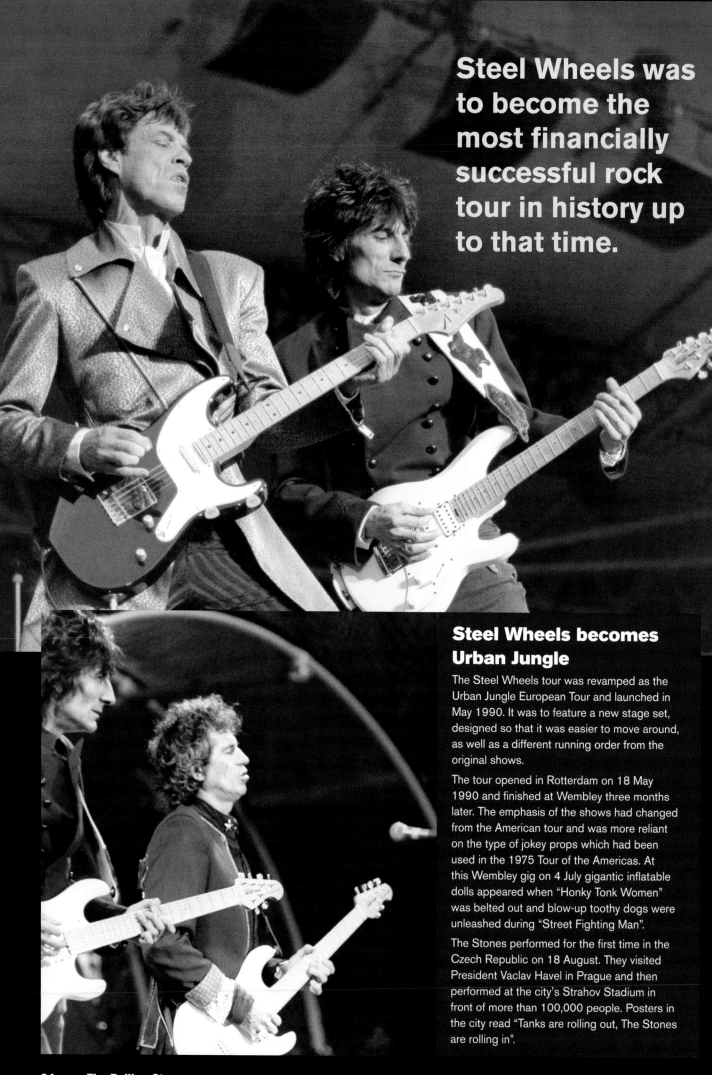

Steel Wheels was to become the most financially successful rock tour in history up to that time.

Steel Wheels becomes Urban Jungle

The Steel Wheels tour was revamped as the Urban Jungle European Tour and launched in May 1990. It was to feature a new stage set, designed so that it was easier to move around, as well as a different running order from the original shows.

The tour opened in Rotterdam on 18 May 1990 and finished at Wembley three months later. The emphasis of the shows had changed from the American tour and was more reliant on the type of jokey props which had been used in the 1975 Tour of the Americas. At this Wembley gig on 4 July gigantic inflatable dolls appeared when "Honky Tonk Women" was belted out and blow-up toothy dogs were unleashed during "Street Fighting Man".

The Stones performed for the first time in the Czech Republic on 18 August. They visited President Vaclav Havel in Prague and then performed at the city's Strahov Stadium in front of more than 100,000 people. Posters in the city read "Tanks are rolling out, The Stones are rolling in".

First trip to Japan

Mick enhanced the sense of theatre through his many costume changes and use of visual effects. The band had taken the Steel Wheels Tour to Japan in February 1990, the first time The Rolling Stones had played there. Their 10 dates at the Tokyo Dome were sold out as the Sports Stadium was transformed into a bleak, monochrome landscape.

Below left: Mick on stage. In March 1990 *Rolling Stone* magazine nominated the band's *Steel Wheels* album for a number of awards including the prestigious best album. The lead single from the album, "Mixed Emotions", was nominated as best single. There were a host of personal nominations for Mick (best male singer), Bill (best bassist) and Charlie (best drummer) as well as accolades for the whole band as best band and artists of 1989.

Timeline 1993

10 Jan Ronnie Wood gives the first of four solo concerts in Japan.

17 Jan Keith Richards' Main Offender tour opens in Seattle.

9 Feb Mick Jagger's third solo album, Wandering Spirit, is released.

16 Feb Bill Wyman stands in for ailing bassist Ronnie Lane at a Faces reunion performance at London's Brit Awards, joining Rod Stewart, Ronnie Wood, Kenney Jones and Ian McLagan onstage.

Apr Mick Jagger and Keith Richards fly to Barbados to begin writing songs for a new album and are shortly joined by Charlie Watts.

9 Jul The band begin recording in Ireland.

12 Oct The Charlie Watts Quintet release their collection Warm & Tender.

28 Nov Virgin release Jump Back, an 18-track greatest hits CD compilation.

1994

Jan Bill Wyman leaves the Rolling Stones. Only three original band members now remain. Bassist Darryl Jones replaces Wyman for the 1994/5 Voodoo Lounge world tour.

The Rolling Stones pick up an MTV Lifetime Achievement Award and a Billboard Award for Artistic Excellence.

The two-year Voodoo Lounge tour opens.

10 Nov The Rolling Stones are the first rock and roll band to broadcast live on the internet.

1995

Jan The South American leg of the tour opens. Shows in South Africa, Japan and Australasia follow.

3 Jun Bob Dylan joins the band onstage in Stockholm for a rendition of 'Like A Rolling Stone'.

30 Aug Tour closes in Rotterdam. Live recordings made during the tour form the album Stripped, released later in the year.

1996

The Rock 'n' Roll Circus album is released. Charlie Watts' quintet release Long Ago And Far Away, an album of jazz and swing classics. Keith Richards works on a solo album.

1997

Aug The Bridges To Babylon tour is announced.

23 Sept Tour opens in Chicago and goes on to thirty-two other cities in North America. Young Leah Wood, Ronnie's daughter, guests with the band when they take the tour to Wembley.

Oct Bill Wyman announces the formation of a new band, The Rhythm Kings. Their first album, Struttin' Our Stuff, features guest musicians Eric Clapton, Albert Lee, Georgie Fame and Peter Frampton.

16 Oct Bill Wyman's first live performance since leaving the Rolling Stones – at the Forum in London.

8 Dec Jerry Hall gives birth to Gabriel Luke Beauregard Jagger in New York – the couple's fourth child and second son.

18 Dec It is announced that so far the Bridges To Babylon tour of North America has grossed nearly $87 million – a box office record.

1998

23 Apr The tour closes with a last show in Chicago – where it had started months earlier.

11 Aug The Rolling Stones play in Moscow for the first time.

2 Nov The album No Security, recorded live at an Amsterdam concert, is released.

1999

Jan Jerry Hall files for divorce from Mick Jagger. In the end she won an annulment as the Bali marriage was not recognised by the courts. Afterwards she said Mick's settlement was 'very generous'.

10 Jun The Rolling Stones play slightly longer than agreed at a small venue in west London and are fined £50,000 for breaching regulations.

27 Jul DNA tests confirm that Mick Jagger is the father of Luciana Morad's baby son, Lucas.

Oct Mick Jagger resumes residence in his former 'marital' home with Jerry Hall. The couple live amicably in separate parts of the house.

13 Nov A re-mix of 'It's Only Rock 'n' Roll' is released as a Christmas single, with proceeds going to charity.

26 Nov A landlord defeats Mick Jagger and Keith Richards in the High Court after the Stones attempt to sue him for exploitation because he named his pub 'Rolling Stone'.

The critically acclaimed *Wandering Spirit* was Mick Jagger's only solo album release of the 1990s.

Solo efforts

Above: Bill holds up a copy of his autobiography *Stone Alone (The Story of a Rock 'n' Roll Band)*, covering the years prior to 1969.

Opposite: Charlie re-launched his tribute to Charlie Parker, *Ode to a High Flying Bird*, at Ronnie Scott's Jazz Club on 3 April 1991. Throughout his career he had derived inspiration from the iconic jazz saxophonist; the Charlie Watts Quintet released two records to honour his hero, *From One Charlie* in February 1991 and *Tribute to Charlie Parker with Strings* in August 1992.

Above right: Mick performs at the Celebration of the Blues concert at the Hammersmith Odeon. Throughout much of 1992 Mick worked in LA on his third solo album *Wandering Spirit*, released in February 1993. The album was a top 20 hit on both sides of the Atlantic and many critics believe it to be his best solo work.

Middle right: Keith performs at the Guitar Legends festival in Seville in October 1991. Earlier in the year the Stones had released the live album, *Flashpoint*, the first live album by the group since 1982's *Still Life (American Concert 1981)*. It had been recorded throughout the Steel Wheels/Urban Jungle tours in 1989 and 1990.

Bottom right: Ronnie Wood was another enthusiastic participant in the Celebration of the Blues concert. He was soon to release his fifth solo album, *Slide on This*. The LP had been partially recorded in Dublin, where U2's iconic guitarist the Edge featured as a guest musician, but it was not a commercial success.

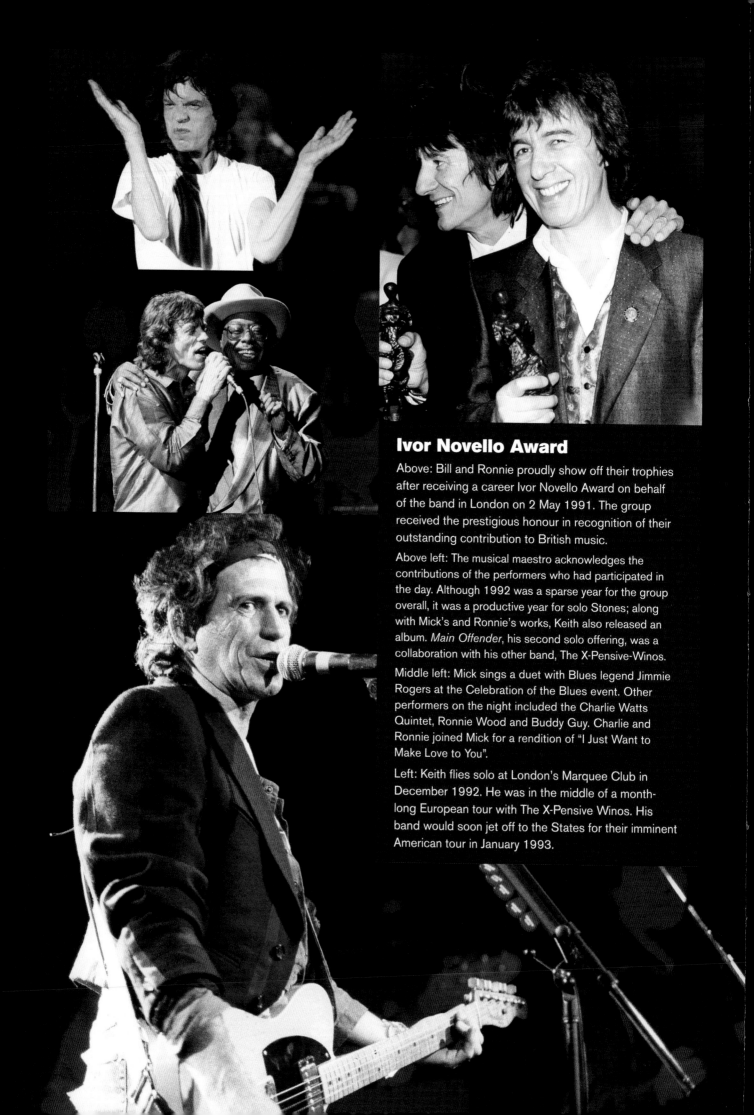

Ivor Novello Award

Above: Bill and Ronnie proudly show off their trophies after receiving a career Ivor Novello Award on behalf of the band in London on 2 May 1991. The group received the prestigious honour in recognition of their outstanding contribution to British music.

Above left: The musical maestro acknowledges the contributions of the performers who had participated in the day. Although 1992 was a sparse year for the group overall, it was a productive year for solo Stones; along with Mick's and Ronnie's works, Keith also released an album. *Main Offender*, his second solo offering, was a collaboration with his other band, The X-Pensive-Winos.

Middle left: Mick sings a duet with Blues legend Jimmie Rogers at the Celebration of the Blues event. Other performers on the night included the Charlie Watts Quintet, Ronnie Wood and Buddy Guy. Charlie and Ronnie joined Mick for a rendition of "I Just Want to Make Love to You".

Left: Keith flies solo at London's Marquee Club in December 1992. He was in the middle of a month-long European tour with The X-Pensive Winos. His band would soon jet off to the States for their imminent American tour in January 1993.

Bill announces his retirement

Above: Bill plays at The Brit Awards at Alexandra Palace in London. On 6 January 1993 he appeared on the TV programme *London Tonight* and announced that he was finally leaving the band saying, "I really don't want to do it anymore. I have many special memories. It's been wonderful. But I thought the last two tours with them were the best we have ever done, so I was quite happy to stop after that." He now continues to tour with his blues rock band, The Rhythm Kings, formed in 1997.

Above right: Ronnie raises his arm aloft at the open-air Hyde Park concert in 1996. Prince Charles watched as the band joined other distinguished musicians including The Who, Bob Dylan and Eric Clapton who had all donated their services in order to raise money for the Prince's Trust.

Voodoo Lounge Tour

Middle right and below: The Voodoo Lounge Tour opened at the Robert F. Kennedy Memorial Stadium in Washington, DC, on 8 August 1994 with Darryl Jones taking the place of Bill Wyman. Following the success of the Steel Wheels/Urban Jungle stage sets, the latest tour again used a technological approach as the band played in front of a huge Jumbotron screen surrounded by a cobra-shaped tower. Banks of lights and the use of pyrotechnics completed the magnificent spectacle.

The theatrical tour included dates in North and South America, South Africa, Japan, New Zealand and Australia before the final leg in Europe started in May 1995. While the tour was in full swing the album *Voodoo Lounge* won the Grammy Award for Best Rock Album in March 1995.

Ladies and Gentlemen: The Rolling Stones

Time is on their side

Above left: The backbone of the Stones' sound, Charlie Watts celebrates his 60th birthday in one of his favourite venues, Ronnie Scott's Jazz Club in Soho, on 2 June 2002. Two years later he was diagnosed with throat cancer and underwent a course of radiotherapy. The cancer is now in remission and he is once again recording and touring with the band.

Middle left: Members of the band at a photocall in Munich during the Licks Tour, which was launched in Toronto in August 2002 and continued for 15 months. It included their first ever concert in Hong Kong.

Below left: Jerry Hall with Bill and Suzanne Wyman. Although both in new relationships, Jerry and Mick remain firm friends intent on bringing up their four children together.

Top: In 2003 "Sir Mick" was knighted for services to music in the Queen's Golden Jubilee Birthday Honours. After the ceremony he posed for photographs with his father Joe and daughters Karis and Elizabeth.

Above: Ronnie Wood at the launch of his new fashion line in October 2009. Although the launch coincided with another recent spell of rehab to tackle his alcohol issues and the divorce from his wife Jo, further success followed with an award for Outstanding Achievement at the Classic Rock Roll of Honour ceremony and the Sony Radio Personality of the Year Award in 2011.

eline 2000

'(I Can't Get No) Satisfaction' topped a US poll of the 100 greatest rock songs of all time.

Mick Jagger returns to his old school Dartford Grammar to open a new arts centre named after him.

Mick, Ronnie, Charlie and Keith play at a private pub gig in south London – a wake for the band's long-term employee Joe Seabrook who died shortly before, aged 58.

Band members convene at the funeral of Eva Jagger, Mick's 87 year-old mother.

Ronnie Wood checks into the Priory Clinic in south London, often used by celebrities keen to kick addictions.

Jade Jagger and her two children survive a car crash near their home in Ibiza.

This year Andrew Loog Oldham's memoirs, Stoned, are published, offering cheerfully unrepentant insights into the Stones' early years. Its author, now a Scientologist and living in Bogota, expresses no regret whatsoever about this parting of the ways with the band he helped to create.

1

Bono, Pete Townsend and Missy Elliott, among others, join Mick Jagger in the studio as he records his next solo album, Goddess In The Doorway.

Mick Jagger announces that the Stones will tour again – but first he has to promote Goddess In The Doorway.

2

A new Rolling Stones tour is announced in New York.

The Rolling Stones Remastered series is announced. Twenty-two classic albums, various compilations and singles will be reformatted for modern home music technology.

The Live Licks tour opens in Toronto. The first leg finishes in Las Vegas in February 2003.

3

Australian leg of the Live Licks tour. It moves to Asia in March, crosses Europe, and finishes with two concerts in Hong Kong in November.

Michael Philip Jagger is knighted for services to music.

4

Charlie Watts is diagnosed with throat cancer. Radiotherapy treatment puts it into remission.

ive Licks, a double live album of the t...... is

2005

26 Jul The band announce plans for their first new album for eight years.

Aug 'Streets of Love' is released as a double A with 'Rough Justice', both from the forthcoming album.

10 Aug A Bigger Bang tour kicks off in Toronto. It covers North and South America, Australasia and Europe, finishing in August 2007.

5 Sept A Bigger Bang is released.

2006

27 Apr Keith Richards suffers a head injury after falling out of a tree on holiday in Fiji, and later undergoes cranial surgey in New Zealand.

Oct/Nov Martin Scorsese films concerts at New York's Beacon Theater. The resulting film, Shine A Light, is released in 2008.

2007

May Premiere of Pirates of the Caribbean: At World's End, in which Keith Richards has a cameo role as Captain Jack Sparrow's father.

10 Jun The Stones appear at the Isle of Wight Festival – their first festival performance for 30 years.

26 Aug Final date of the A Bigger Bang tour at the O2 Arena in London.

2 Oct Mick Jagger releases a compilation of his solo work, The Very Best of Mick Jagger.

2008

1 Apr Shine a Light, the soundtrack to the Scorsese film, is released and debuts at No.2 in the UK charts.

Jul Ronnie Wood leaves his wife of 23 years for a young Russian model.

2009

25 Oct Bill Wyman fills in for the late Ronnie Lane at a Faces reunion concert, performing alongside Ronnie Wood.

2010

17 Apr 'Plundered My Soul' is released as a limited edition single in honour of Record Store Day.

23 May Exile On Main Street is reissued and goes straight to No.1 again in the UK charts.

Sept Ronnie Wood releases his seventh solo album, I Feel Like Playing.

11 Oct Ladies and Gentlemen: The Rolling Stones is released in cinemas and later on to DVD. A digitally remastered version of the film was shown in select theatres across the US.

26 Oct Publication of Keith Richards' memoirs, Life

Time – for the greatest of all rock and roll bands – is still on their side...

Bigger Bang tour

The 24-month Bigger Bang tour began in Toronto in August 2005 and took in 146-dates worldwide including a free concert on Copacabana Beach which attracted an estimated audience of 2 million. During a six-week break from the tour, Richards fell from a tree in Fiji and had surgery to remove a blood clot from his brain, but soon made a full recovery. It eventually became the second highest grossing tour in history with takings in excess of $500 million.

Overleaf top: The mammoth set, designed by Mark Fisher, included a 25-metre-high stage with balconies to accommodate an additional 400 spectators. State-of-the-art electronics broadcast live footage to the

12 July 2012 marked the 50th anniversary of the Stones' debut as the Rollin' Stones at the Marquee Club in London in 1962. The band marked the occasion by attending the private view of a photographic exhibition at Somerset House that documented their 50-year career. Later Mick Jagger confirmed that they had been invited to appear at the London 2012 Olympic Games Opening Ceremony but had decided that they were not yet 'stage ready' – although they were currently rehearsing together again in the hopes of appearing live later in the year to celebrate their anniversary.

After a break of more than five years the Rolling Stones, along with special guests Bill Wyman and Mick Taylor, finally appeared live at a major venue – on 25 November 2012 the O2 Arena in London hosted the first of six concerts to celebrate the Stones' 50th anniversary. Fans had come from all over the world to hear hits from across the last five decades and – despite a minimum price of more than £100 – tickets for the two UK concerts sold out within seven minutes.

The two London concerts were followed by four in America, one at the Barclays Center and one at Madison Square Garden in New York and two at the Prudential Center in Newark, New Jersey. Bill did not play at these, but Mick Taylor again made a guest appearance

Timeline 2011

13 Feb   Mick Jagger performs live at the Grammy Awards in Los Angeles for the first time.

11 Apr   An Ian Stewart tribute album, Boogie 4 Stu, features The Rolling Stones with Bill Wyman for the first time in 20 years, performing Bob Dylan's 'Watchin' the River Flow'.

Jul   Release of the first single, 'Miracle Worker' by Mick Jagger and his new group SuperHeavy.

26 Aug   Keith Richard's book Life sells one million copies and in November he was awarded the Mailer Prize for Distinguished Biography.

21 Nov   The 1978 album Some Girls is re-released in an expanded and remastered edition.

2012

12 Jul   50th anniversary of the first official appearance of the Rolling Stones at the Marquee Club in London in 1962.

18 Oct   World première of the film Crossfire Hurricane, which documents the Rolling Stones' career from the 1960s to the current day.

25 Nov   The Stones play the O2 Arena in London, their first official live performance together for five years. They were joined for two songs by Bill Wyman and for another by Mick Taylor.

8 Dec   First of four US concerts takes place in New York.

2013

3 May   The 50 and Counting Tour officially kicks off with a concert at the Staples Center in Los Angeles.

29 Jun   The Rolling Stones appear for the first time at Glastonbury Festival, on the Pyramid Stage. The day before Bill Wyman had appeared with his Rhythm Kings on the acoustic stage.

6 Jul   The Rolling Stones perform the first of two concerts in Hyde Park; the second was on 13 July.

1 Nov   The Ronnie Wood Band perform at BluesFest 2013 at the Royal Albert Hall, London.

2014

21 Feb   The 14 on Fire Tour begins with a concert at du Arena, Yas Island, in Abu Dhabi. Dates are confirmed for venues across Asia and Australasia.

50 & Counting

Below: The Air Canada Centre in Toronto was one of the venues during the nineteen-date North American lef of the 50 & Counting Tour in spring 2013. Five dates in Asia and seven in Australasia have been announced for the 14 On Fire tour in spring 2014.

Opposite below: Surprisingly the Stones had never played Glastonbury, but 2013 was to remedy this – on 29 June they appeared on the famous Pyramid Stage in front of over 130,000 festival goers. After a performance that lasted over two hours and covered most of their major hits as well as a few esoteric song choices, it was generally agreed that the Rolling Stones had confirmed their reputation as 'the greatest rock 'n' roll band in the world'.